P9-CDA-657

Praise for *Engagement Marketing*

"This book is for small business owners who want to learn how to leverage the power of online and offline communication to grow their business. It offers a refreshing look at how any business can grow by engaging with their customers. It's not about tweets or Likes. It's about doing right by your customers and enabling them to let others know about it. This book helps you do this in very practical terms. This book is a must-read for any business owner who is tired of the song and dance of 'content,' tone deaf to social media, and sick of blogging. This book is for those who want the 'steak' and not 'oatmeal' of making customers, loyal customers."

—Ramon Ray, Technology Evangelist and Editor, Smallbiztechnology.com

"*Engagement Marketing* lives the talk with practical examples from small businesses on how to excel in their business with online content and make it easy for customers to interact with the business. Gail Goodman uses the power of storytelling to explain online marketing in the easiest and grassroots terms."

—Shashi Bellamkonda, Senior Director, Social Media, Network Solutions and Adjunct Faculty Member at Georgetown University

"If you're a small business owner you probably know Constant Contact. In her new book, CEO Gail Goodman takes you further down the road to success. The old values are still the best values and Gail has given them new life for the Internet age. She helps entrepreneurs understand that Main Street isn't dead, it just went digital. Throughout, you'll learn how to put the 'word-of-mouth' power of social media to your advantage. Small business owners who want to survive and thrive in the new world of Yelping and blogging need to read this book."

—Charles "Tee" Rowe, President and CEO, Association of Small Business Development Centers (ASBDC)

"This book is a must-read for any small business owner looking to understand the latest trend in permission-based marketing—permission to engage. When done well, it brings small businesses new customers from their existing ones. Gail Goodman makes a strong case for how *Engagement Marketing* will become an incredibly important source of new customers for small businesses—the key to growing in any economy. Best of all, she explains how *Engagement Marketing* gets 'done' in very practical terms, using a combination of old and new online marketing tools, including e-mail and social media."

—JJ Ramberg, Host of MSNBC's "Your Business"

"Businesses that have a loyal and engaged customer base enjoy greater success. Why? Because educated consumers seek those companies that listen to their needs, and when they find them, not only do they stick, but they also share their experiences with others. It's a marketing strategy known as engagement marketing, and no one is more of an expert than Gail Goodman. In her book, Gail shares the important strategies all businesses can employ to leverage technology and social media platforms to build their businesses. This is absolutely a must-read for any owner or team that is struggling to survive. Gail's sage advice will turn your business into a thriving entity, and you'll soar to success.

—Susan Solovic, CEO and Cofounder, ItsYourBiz.com,
New York Times* Best-Selling Author of *It's Your Biz:
The Complete Guide to Becoming Your Own Boss

"*Engagement Marketing*, as clearly explained by Gail Goodman, will help businesses face the public in personal, human ways. That connection is what chambers of commerce do, too; at least they should. Those who read the book will know better how to reach out to their community and their current and potential customers."

—Mick Fleming, President and CEO,
American Chamber of Commerce
Executives (ACCE)

ENGAGEMENT MARKETING

ENGAGEMENT MARKETING

How Small Business Wins in a Socially Connected World

Gail F. Goodman

WILEY

John Wiley & Sons, Inc.

Published by John Wiley & Sons, Inc., Hoboken, New Jersey.
Published simultaneously in Canada.

For general information on our other products and services or for technical support, please contact our Customer Care Department within the United States at (800) 762-2974, outside the United States at (317) 572-3993 or fax (317) 572-4002.

Wiley publishes in a variety of print and electronic formats and by print-on-demand. Some material included with standard print versions of this book may not be included in e-books or in print-on-demand. If this book refers to media such as a CD or DVD that is not included in the version you purchased, you may download this material at http://booksupport.wiley.com. For more information about Wiley products, visit www.wiley.com.

Library of Congress Cataloging-in-Publication Data:

Goodman, Gail F., 1960-
 Engagement marketing : how small business wins in a socially connected world / Gail F. Goodman.
  p. cm.
 Includes index.
 ISBN 978-1-118-10102-5 (cloth); ISBN 978-1-118-22378-9 (ebk);
 ISBN 978-1-118-23711-3 (ebk); ISBN 978-1-118-26208-5 (ebk)
  1. Internet marketing. 2. Small business marketing. 3. Online social networks. 4. Social media. I. Title.
 HF5415.1265.G659 2012
 658.8'72—dc23

                                                                2012003556

Printed in the United States of America
10 9 8 7 6 5 4 3 2

This book is dedicated to small businesses and organizations everywhere. Your dreams, passion, creativity, tenacity, and guts continually inspire me.

Contents

Chapter 8
Engagement Marketing Tips and Tricks

Learn five easy-to-implement social word-of-mouth methods
that take only a few minutes each day but deliver real impact
in the form of increased engagement and visibility, leading to
increased business.

Chapter 9
Overcoming Common Obstacles

Find time in today's crazy busy world to implement
your Engagement Marketing Cycle by using the
tools and tactics you already have.

Chapter 10
Resources

Tools, tips, and tricks to help you take your
Engagement Marketing to the next level.

FOREWORD

A few years ago, we did a survey of small businesses and found that 83 percent said their main source of new business was "referrals."

Think about that statistic for a moment. As a small business owner, your new business most often comes from other people who are talking about your company. And who are those "other people"? Complete strangers? People who've never heard of your business? Of course not!

The people who recommend your business to others are those who already know your business. They have had a positive experience with your business. They feel so positive that they *want* to tell others about it. Those people are, in two words . . . your customers.

The people spreading the word are current or past customers who, when asked which company they recommend, have such a warm and fuzzy feeling (in marketing speak, they are "highly satisfied") that your company's name is the first out of their mouths. They don't have to think long and hard about it. It pops out spontaneously. Your business is top-of-mind.

Highly satisfied customers often don't wait for anyone to ask. They may be so wowed by their experience that they rave about it over lunch with colleagues or at networking events. They might even volunteer how happy they are with your product or service by writing about it on their company blog or personal Twitter account. Or perhaps, if they think that your company really went above and beyond, they'll leave a five-star review on one of the many consumer review sites.

Whatever they do, they are telling others about your business in such a way that it leads to new customers and more sales.

OUR ENDLESS QUEST FOR NEW CUSTOMERS

We business owners and marketers tend to obsess over new customers. A friend of mine calls the quest for new customers the "Holy Grail of small business." It's the pot of gold at the end of the rainbow. It's the buried treasure we seek.

A question I hear over and over in my interactions with other business owners is "How do I get new customers for my business?"

We see this question covered daily in the blogosphere. On social media sites such as Twitter and Facebook, small business owners endlessly share tips about how to get new customers. We hear the topic discussed in person at conferences and industry events.

We small business owners talk with colleagues (though not competitors, of course!) about how to get customers. We may advertise to bring in new customers or offer special promotions and discounts. We invest in search engine optimization to direct new people to visit our websites or blogs, hoping they'll find us online and get directions to our physical locations. We use Google AdWords to drive new customers to our eCommerce stores. We attend conferences to learn how to drive new sales. We may retain a business coach to help motivate us and our sales team to find new customers. We may even devour books in our spare time . . . books about how to sell to new customers.

Think of all the effort and brainpower we've put toward finding new customers.

Yet, how many of us devote a significant chunk of our resources—time, money, and staff—to actively engage with our *existing customers*? What do we do to increase the warm and fuzzy, highly satisfied feeling among the very people who are talking about our businesses, spreading that word of mouth that leads to new customers and keeps existing customers coming back?

And how many of us know exactly where our referrals are coming from? Do we make any effort to track the source of referrals and encourage them?

Most of us, I suspect, could do much, much more.

The need to engage with existing customers has become even more urgent over the past decade, because so much discussion happens online. With the explosion of social media sites, such as Facebook, Twitter, and Google+, and review sites like Yelp and TripAdvisor, it's easier than ever for a satisfied—or dissatisfied—customer to spread the word about your business. And does it spread! Even if you are certain that most of your business comes from your local community, whether you realize it or not, people may be discussing on the Web the experience they had with your business.

ENTER ENGAGEMENT MARKETING

That's where *Engagement Marketing: How Small Business Wins in a Socially Connected World* comes in. Engagement Marketing refers to providing a great experience and encouraging your customers to tell your story through socially visible word-of-mouth referrals.

As Gail Goodman points out in this book, Engagement Marketing is a cycle. She shows you how to engage your customers online to drive more new leads, more repeat sales, and more referrals.

It's all part of one loop, and when you get good at Engagement Marketing, you'll sell more.

The Engagement Marketing Cycle consists of three steps:

- Deliver a WOW! experience so that customers will remember your business with a positive feeling.

- Entice customers to stay in touch, whether via e-mail marketing or social media, so that they'll give you permission to continue to stay connected and market to them.

- Engage people through social media, e-mail newsletters, blog posts, and other methods to keep them interested and help them find value in staying connected.

Engagement Marketing is marketing, true. But it's not traditional marketing in the sense of unrelentingly pushing "buy now" offers on your current customers. Do that and you'll soon turn people off.

Rather, Engagement Marketing is about making your company so interesting and providing so much value that people *want* to stay connected and maintain a relationship. By doing so, you greatly increase the likelihood of existing customers talking positively about your business on social channels and thinking of your company when it's time to buy again or they are asked for a referral.

If you own a small business, or you're a marketer or sales executive challenged with increasing sales in your company, this is a book you can't afford not to read. You won't be presented with baffling technospeak about social media sites. Instead, you will get the straight scoop delivered in easy-to-understand business terminology. And you get practical advice that you can put to work no matter what size your business.

—**Anita Campbell**,
CEO and Publisher of Small Business Trends website

INTRODUCTION

I'm an amateur chef (emphasis on "amateur"), and my husband and I enjoy entertaining and having people over to our home. I had needed to replace my knives for some time, so I went to Kitchen Outfitters, a local kitchen store, to see what was available. A little overwhelmed at the selection of knives and brands, I asked the shop owner a few questions. She took the time to explain the difference between German and Japanese knives and even pulled out a chopping board and proceeded to let me try the different knives by cutting up carrots. Sold! I ended up buying six well-made knives. Each time I have guests over and we are cooking together, I tell them about my knives and how wonderfully sharp they are, which leads me to tell them the story of my great experience with Kitchen Outfitters.

What's key here is that I've shared my experience (multiple times!) via word of mouth. Word-of-mouth referrals aren't new, of course. We've always relied on our friends, family, and coworkers for referrals. Maybe the trees in your yard need pruning or you need a new roof, so you ask your neighbors or coworkers which companies they've used in the past. Or it's your 10-year wedding anniversary, and you really want to wow your spouse, so you ask around for recommendations to some of the better restaurants in your area. Word of mouth has always worked, and it still works.

What's changed, however, is how we solicit these referrals. We still ask our friends, family, and coworkers for their feedback and share our experiences with them, but now we're using technology to do it.

As a small business owner or marketer, you've seen firsthand the extraordinary changes that technology and social media have wrought, from the ubiquitous Facebook "Like" button and real-time tweets of global events to Yelp reviews and YouTube videos. Thanks to social media and its nimble partner, mobile technology, it's now easier than ever for people to gain instant insight into news, events, people—and your business—by simply turning to their online networks and the collective experiences of others found on public review sites.

As a consumer and a businessperson, I, too, rely on my network and social media channels for information. I no longer go into a new restaurant, for example, without first checking the reviews at OpenTable or Yelp. And as a CEO, I no longer hire professional services firms without first checking with my network comprised of current and ex-colleagues and my CEO peers. As I write this, a friend in my network is moving to a new accounting firm. He used LinkedIn to ask if any of us had experience working with the firm and audit partner that he's considering. He's also doing social media searches to see what others have to say.

It's easy to focus on social media and new technology as the marketing game changers, especially since the use of mobile devices, such as smartphones and tablets, is rising rapidly. However, smartphones are not what have changed the game.

What's the real marketing game changer? Age-old word-of-mouth marketing strategies made *publicly visible* by social media sites. Word-of-mouth referrals, which used to happen between neighbors over the back fence, at cocktail parties, business functions, and your children's birthday parties, are now visible to your customers and your prospects. With today's social media tools, your customers can post reviews, endorse businesses using the "Like" and "share" buttons, and talk about brands on platforms such as Twitter, LinkedIn, Google+, and YouTube for the entire world to see. Businesses can engage their customers in LinkedIn Groups or on blogs. Your customers now have a voice that can be heard beyond their immediate circle of close friends and family.

And that's what this book is about: leveraging your existing customers' "voice" to help you grow your business.

"WHAT DO WE DO WITH SOCIAL MEDIA?"

Most of the small businesses we've talked to over the years (small businesses being the bulk of the Constant Contact user base) have two huge priorities: one, they want to find new customers; and two, they want to get the biggest bang for their marketing dollars and time invested. These were the concerns that we used to hear, and still hear, over and over at our small business seminars and workshops. But as social media emerged, we began hearing new concerns:

"Why should my customers care about what I had for breakfast?"

"I don't understand how Facebook can benefit my business. Isn't it just for kids?"

"Do we *really* need to pay attention to this? I don't have the time."

As social media continued to gain momentum and people began experimenting, they shared their success stories as well as their challenges. Healthy discussions blossomed as business owners investigated how social media could drive the most impact.

These questions were also driving deeper and lengthier conversations among us at Constant Contact—questions that prompted us to step back and think about the challenges and opportunities of social media. Was social media a fundamental change in marketing or just a new way of getting our marketing messages out? We kept talking and sharing and listening and realized that something was *very* different—but this difference wasn't about the technology or the tools. It was about a new marketing concept . . . what we call *Engagement Marketing*.

ENGAGEMENT MARKETING: MAKING MAGIC HAPPEN

Engagement Marketing is about getting new customers through your existing customers while driving more repeat sales at the same time. Engagement Marketing builds on the tried-and-true basics of building your business—namely, the importance of happy customers driving referrals. But now, with the addition of the social media megaphone, you as a business owner can drive more dramatic results with a lot less effort. This is because social media enables a different level of customer engagement, one that you can use to encourage and reward customer conversations— conversations that include positive mentions and endorsements, as seen in this Twitter exchange between Boloco fan @ajmadsen203 and Cassidy at Boloco:

> @boloco Thank you for the greatest breakfast burrito I've ever had, it's gunna get me thru hump day.
>
> @ajmadsen203 aww ur welcome! what kind did u get? have a good #humpday! ^cassidy

There are two great outcomes from this exchange. First, @ajmadsen203's followers hear a ringing endorsement of Boloco and their breakfast burritos. Maybe they have never tried Boloco, and this is the nudge they need. Or maybe they've never thought about a burrito spot as a breakfast choice! The second outcome is that Boloco's response reinforced @ajmadsen203's loyalty.

If you're a small retail business, you probably already know your regular customers. I know that many of the local establishments with whom I do business know me by name. But what they don't know is what I say about them to others. It's difficult to track or reward your customers for promoting your business to friends and family "in real life." You can use loyalty marketing to reward customers for coming back, but it's not as easy to reward them for referring you, and it's even harder to track these referrals.

Engagement Marketing, on the other hand, allows you to encourage your customers to engage and interact with you as if you are neighbors chatting across the back fence. By engaging your customers, you derive two benefits: You make your customers part of your marketing team, and it's this visible engagement and the positive endorsements that will bring you tomorrow's customers. Not only do your current customers and fans influence how others perceive your brand, they also help build the trust needed to get others to do business with you. The difference is that these valuable endorsers, who have always existed, are now in plain sight, ready for you to nurture, engage, and reward.

WHO SHOULD READ THIS BOOK

In this book, you'll learn why Engagement Marketing is a real opportunity for fostering deeper connections with your customers, which in turn will drive new business. I can name dozens of books on how to use social media. This isn't one of them. While I'll cover social media tools and how to use them, this information will always be presented in the context of building and sustaining genuine connections with customers.

This book is for anyone who owns or works for a small business or organization, whether you sell to consumers or businesses or run a nonprofit organization or association. Whether you want to find more new customers, drive more repeat sales, bring in new members, or raise more money for your nonprofit, you will benefit from reading this book. In the first section, you'll learn about the Engagement Marketing Cycle and how it works. In the second part, you'll find case studies and practical tips for maximizing your Engagement Marketing opportunities.

I don't have to tell you that social media networks, tools, and technologies are rapidly changing. In this book, you will find concepts that transcend the changing technologies, so if some of the examples are a bit dated by the time you read this, forgive us and focus on the message.[1] I also encourage you to visit the companion site to this book, engagementmarketing.com. You'll find tips, case studies, and more. Be sure to pay a visit!

We here at Constant Contact see firsthand how many small businesses are thriving, thanks to simple techniques such as combining social media with e-mail marketing. I get excited about the fact that while marketing is changing, these changes allow you to reach your customers and connect with them on a personal level in a way you just couldn't do even five years ago. I know, because many of the small business owners and marketers we work with are now using Engagement Marketing to grow their businesses— and you'll read a few of their stories in this book. If it can work for them, it can work for you, too.

---

[1] As this book was going to press, Facebook announced that it was replacing PageWalls with Timelines, so all references to Wall in this book are equivalent to Timeline.

Part I

Rev Up Your Engagement Marketing Engine

CHAPTER 1

THE ENGAGEMENT MARKETING CYCLE

A couple traveled to the Boston area to attend a wedding, and their host—who lived in the area—booked them a room at a gorgeous bed and breakfast. The B&B's website featured fabulous photography of its stunning location, so the bride felt good about choosing this particular B&B. She requested a room on the first floor and informed the person handling the reservation that the husband had trouble climbing stairs due to a physical disability.

When the couple arrived, they learned that no first floor rooms were available; instead, they had been given a room two flights up at the back of the B&B. You know how this works. You don't like to make a fuss, so you say, "Okay, we'll deal with it." The room, although difficult to access, was lovely. After attending the wedding, however, the couple returned to their room to find a freshly made bed . . . and a pile of wet towels on the floor. When the couple reported the mess to the front desk receptionist, they got a blank stare and a shoulder shrug.

This is the negative TripAdvisor.com review that I—and thousands of others like me—read about the B&B "[that] didn't care enough to give us a first floor room even though one was specifically requested due to physical disability." I found this review while looking for a place for friends to stay while visiting my town. Do you think I booked a room at this B&B? No! And I'm willing to bet that many other viewers followed suit.

Compare this to a grateful bride's positive review of an inn in Connecticut. The couple's wedding reception had to be rescheduled at the last minute due to a hurricane. The inn owners helped plan the reception right down "to the last detail" and even hosted the entire bridal party. The bride praised the staff, the food, and the grounds and raved, "We'll definitely be back! Thank you!!" Think about how many bookings the inn may receive from other brides seeking exceptional service and a worry-free wedding day—all thanks to one glowing review.

When we ask business owners, "What is the single most effective source for generating new customers?" the most common answer is, "My customers telling others about me."

EVERYONE HAS A CIRCLE OF INFLUENCE

Whether we join to build professional relationships (e.g., industry associations) or for more personal reasons (e.g., parenting groups, lifestyles, similar hobbies or interests, alumni associations, and so on), we all belong to various networks. These groups include our close and extended family, personal friends, acquaintances, colleagues, neighbors, and coworkers, to name just a few. Usually, our networks are filled with people like us—whether we belong to a group of new mothers or a group of serial entrepreneurs. Our networks, which can be forged online or offline, form our circle of influence; we influence them and they influence us.

When we get together with our peers within these groups, we share information and updates about our personal and professional lives. Think about the last time you caught up with a friend or family member. You probably discussed what your kids and spouse are up to or where you went on your last vacation.

Similarly, when you last attended an industry association meeting, you most likely shared resources, anecdotes, news, and business challenges with other small business owners or marketers in your industry. If one of your peers asked, "Say, do you know of a marketing consultant? We need help with developing an online marketing strategy," you may have said, "Actually I do. You'll want to call Jane Smith. She does great work—five stars."

This word-of-mouth referral is the golden moment for a business or consultant, but several factors make it difficult to encourage or track: (1) You can't influence how your business is portrayed in the conversation; (2) You have no idea when someone refers a friend to you unless that friend calls to inquire about your services and you happen to ask how he or she found you; and (3) You can't reward your clients for referring you if you don't even know who made the referral.

Social media completely changes this scenario.

In the days before social media and the Internet, you, the business owner, could not listen in on your customers' conversations about your company. Nor could you easily encourage people to spread the good word about your business unless you used loyalty marketing or a "tell a friend" campaign, both of which are expensive to conduct and maintain.

With today's social media tools at your disposal, you can encourage your clients to tell your story for you through Engagement Marketing. Engagement Marketing is built on a simple yet powerful idea: When you connect with your customers online, you stop speaking *to* your customers and start talking *with* them, and wonderful things begin to happen. Those golden word-of-mouth moments that once happened in the backyard, at parties, and at networking events suddenly begin happening right in front of your eyes on Facebook, LinkedIn, Twitter, and review sites. Through Engagement Marketing, word-of-mouth referrals become socially amplified: your customers' friends, families, and networks all see these referrals and beat a path to your door.

YOUR NEW BUSINESS ENGINE: NEW CUSTOMERS AND MORE REPEAT BUSINESS

Engagement Marketing helps drive more leads, more repeat sales—and more referrals. Engagement Marketing stimulates conversations and inspires participation. As you engage with your customers (and their friends), you'll achieve surprisingly targeted social visibility; your customers' networks are filled with great prospects for you. Remember, we're all part of networks filled with people like us, so we all tend to have friends and colleagues with similar needs. When a friend of a friend finds your business through a trusted connection, it comes with the explicit or implied endorsement that this person stands behind your business. This endorsement gives you greater reach and adds to your credibility—or "social proof"—as prospects that find you through other channels can easily see your positive engagement with returning customers.

Your customers' testimonials carry more credibility than any marketing message you could ever deliver yourself. This is because we value the feedback of others more than a vendor's claims. If we actually know the person who is giving positive (or negative!) feedback, the review's credibility skyrockets. In fact, 90 percent of consumers trust recommendations from people they know[1] while only 14 percent trust advertising.[2]

---

[1]Nielsen Wire blog, July 7, 2009, http://blog.nielsen.com/nielsenwire/consumer/global-advertising-consumers-trust-real-friends-and-virtual-strangers-the-most.
[2]Socialnomics, May 5, 2010, www.socialnomics.net/2010/05/05/social-media-revolution-2-refresh.

THE ENGAGEMENT MARKETING CYCLE: THREE SIMPLE STEPS TO SUCCESS

The Engagement Marketing Cycle begins once you've attracted a prospective customer or client to your business, as represented by the door in Figure 1.1. This first point of contact can happen at your physical location, website, Facebook Page, trade show booth, charity event—anywhere you make a connection with someone and the conversation turns to business.

The Engagement Marketing Cycle, as seen in Figure 1.2, is comprised of three simple steps: Experience, Entice, and Engage. Although relatively simple, these three steps, when done right, are quite powerful. What follows is a brief description of the cycle. You'll find more in-depth information on each step, plus practical tips, in the following chapters.

Offline

Online

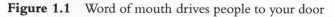
Word of Mouth Drives People to Your Door.

OPEN

Figure 1.1 Word of mouth drives people to your door

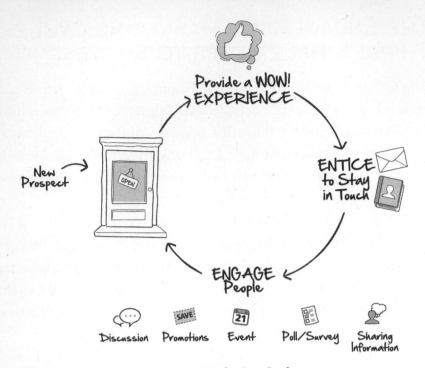

Figure 1.2   The Engagement Marketing Cycle

Step 1: Provide a WOW! Experience

The good news is that as a small business, you have an advantage that larger or national companies do not: you can create personal connections with your customers by providing extraordinary *experiences*—every single day. These experiences include everything from remembering your customers' names and preferences to providing them with exceptional service they just do not get anywhere else. Creating a great customer experience from the moment a prospective or existing customer enters your business is crucial to revving up your Engagement Marketing engine. As Figure 1.3 shows, your goal at this step in the cycle is to deliver a positive, memorable customer experience that stays alive in your customers' memories long after they have exited your business.

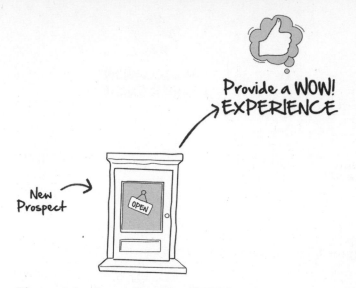

Figure 1.3 Step 1: Provide a WOW! experience

I don't have to tell you that the bar is set pretty low in many businesses when it comes to creating great customer experiences. According to the 2011 Global Customer Service Barometer Research Report prepared by American Express, only 24 percent of survey respondents said that businesses "will go the extra mile."[3] Almost half of the respondents, or 42 percent, said the businesses are helpful but don't "do anything extra to keep [my] business," while 22 percent said that companies "take [my] business for granted."

Clearly, businesses can step it up with regard to providing exceptional service. As a small business owner, you have an advantage: you can easily assess your customer experience and implement necessary changes faster than large businesses can, and the rewards—new and repeat business—appear fairly quickly. Great customer experiences fuel the Engagement Marketing Cycle; without them, you won't get the cycle started. In Chapter 2, we'll explore ways to create great customer experiences.

[3]http://about.americanexpress.com/news/pr/2010/barometer.aspx.

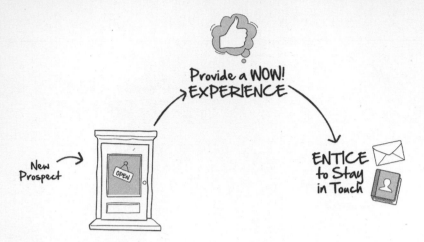

Figure 1.4   Step 2: Entice to stay in touch

Step 2: Entice to Stay in Touch

When you create a great customer experience, you make it easier for customers to be receptive to doing business with you again, to remaining in touch with you, and to sharing their experiences with their networks. But you can't keep that great experience alive, if you have no way to stay in touch! You need to make a connection while the experience is fresh in their minds. To this end, you must persuade the customer to agree or "opt in" to staying connected. For this second step in the Engagement Marketing Cycle to work as shown in Figure 1.4, you must learn how to connect with your customers through a variety of media including social networks, e-mail, mobile (SMS or texting), events and, yes, even direct mail. Once you decide how you want to connect, you have to *entice* your customers to make the connection (often called opt in). Creating opportunities and methods for enticing new customers to connect with you is limited only by your imagination and creativity. E-mail marketing and social media platforms (such as your blog, Facebook, LinkedIn, Google+, YouTube, and Twitter) tied specifically to your business are the two most frequently used methods for maintaining connections.

In Chapter 3 you'll learn how to comfortably ask people to connect with your business and entice them to opt in. The key takeaway is this: consider how you can entice people to connect with you during or immediately after they've done business with you.

Step 3: Engage People

Now that you've delivered a great customer *experience* and have *enticed* customers to stay in touch, it's time to bring these relationships to life by *engaging* people, as seen in Figure 1.5. "Engagement" means sharing content that inspires your fans, followers, e-mail subscribers, blog readers, and other online contacts to interact with you. Creating opportunities for engagement brings customers back to your business—by leaving a comment, "Liking" or "1+-ing" your post or website, sharing your content on Facebook,

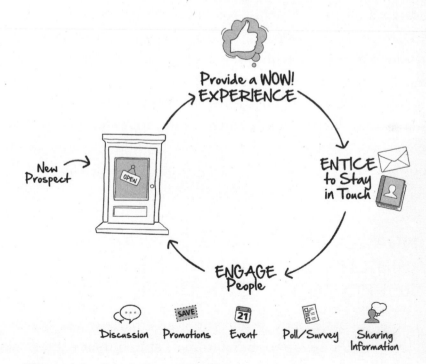

Figure 1.5   Step 3: Engage People

Twitter, Google+, or LinkedIn, visiting your business to make a purchase, or calling/e-mailing you to discuss a new project.

Engaging with people is not a one-way street. If all your audience does is listen to you, then you're not fully engaging them. The goal is to drive participation, whether online or off, and social media is particularly well suited to encouraging online engagement. Facebook, Twitter, LinkedIn, Google+, YouTube, and a company blog provide you with the ability to create a destination for viewer interaction and establish a shared interest community. E-mail marketing is a great way to pull people back to your social networks. When your audience participates, especially on social networks, it creates buzz around you and your business: When your customers "Like," comment, or share stories, their participation becomes visible to their networks (your new prospects!).

Chapter 4 outlines the basic types of content that engage people and explains how you can use content to drive active participation.

That closes the loop on the Engagement Marketing Cycle. Developing this cycle until it's a well-oiled machine will keep your customers and clients connected to your business, increasing your repeat sales. Engagement Marketing, however, has an even bigger benefit: Engagement leads to endorsement—that golden word-of-mouth moment that drives new customers to your business.

ENGAGEMENT DRIVES SOCIAL VISIBILITY, ATTRACTING NEW PROSPECTS TO YOUR DOOR

We opened the chapter with examples of negative and positive reviews on TripAdvisor.com. Customers shared their experiences with a subpar bed and breakfast and an excellent inn—reviews that are visible to everyone who logs on to the site. But reviews are just one way that customers share their experiences. When you engage your customers through social media in a way that drives participation, you create *socially visible* actions. On social networks, your customer interactions are visible to other customers and prospects. When someone "Likes" or follows your business, comments on your posts, or shares your content with their networks, those actions are visible. When people tweet about your upcoming event or share that they are at your establishment, those actions are socially visible. When you engage in a way that drives participation, you create socially visible actions. In Chapter 6, we will explain in further detail how customer participation becomes visible across each of the social networks.

As shown in Figure 1.6 socially visible engagement puts your business or organization in front of a new audience: the social networks of your existing customers. Not only are they seeing and hearing about your business, they are hearing about it from a trusted source, giving you an implicit thumbs-up.

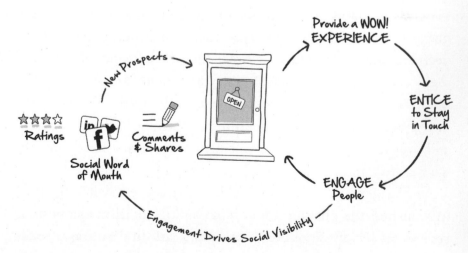

Figure 1.6   The Engagement Marketing Cycle with social visibility

Engagement Marketing Boosts Your Other Marketing, Too

Socially visible engagement can have a big impact on your other sales and marketing efforts. A person who gets your direct mail letter or reads your ad and then looks you up online can see the engagement of your fans on Facebook, the comments on your blog, the mentions on Twitter and LinkedIn, and can know immediately that you're a business that listens to its customers. This positive engagement—or social proof, which we discuss in later chapters—encourages people to connect with you, especially if someone they know (i.e., friends and family) are engaging with you, too. As we'll discuss, social proof helps build trust and is much more powerful than any marketing message you can put out. Engagement Marketing helps you close new business by giving your prospects confidence.

Engagement Marketing Builds Momentum Over Time

When you follow the three-step Engagement Marketing Cycle, magic starts to happen and takes many forms. Our highly connected digital world makes it easier than ever for people to share their experiences with their networks (and strangers!); social media tools allow for these experiences to be spread far and wide. You'll begin to see existing customers coming back more often, and over time, you'll begin to meet their friends. This interaction starts slowly and builds gradually.

As engagement begins to build, you'll see explicit references to your business popping up in blogs and in social media posts as well as on review sites. New customers will find you as a result of an inquiry that someone posted online, which resulted in a recommendation for your business. Someone will post on Twitter or Facebook, or in a discussion group ("Does anybody know of a great housepainter in San Leandro, California?") and your engaged customers will hop in and recommend you. This discussion stream has the potential to be seen by all of the conversation's participants as well as their entire networks. When you consider that the average Facebook user has 120 friends[4] you quickly realize how many people can be reached with just one posting.

This is the magic of a well-functioning Engagement Marketing Cycle; it drives both new prospects and repeat sales. Once the Engagement Marketing cycle is fully functioning, your customers become part of your marketing team. The cycle now becomes a new customer acquisition engine while also strengthening the sources you already use.

Are you ready to build your engine? Let's get started with the first step in the cycle: Providing a WOW! experience.

---

[4]Facebook, 2009, www.facebook.com/note.php?note_id=55257228858.

CHAPTER 2

DELIVER A WOW!
EXPERIENCE

"The straps frayed on my Yakima bike rack, so I contacted the company to order new straps under warranty. A couple of weeks passed and no straps. I contacted Yakima again and was told that the straps were back-ordered and that it might take awhile to order them. To soften the disappointment, they sent me, free of charge, a brand new bike rack second-day air! I'm a Yakima customer for life."

—*Joe Simone*

As a small business owner, you already know that delivering a great customer experience accelerates your success. In addition to driving repeat business, these experiences generate positive referrals, bringing you more business. We call these the Three Rs: Rave Reviews, Repeat Business, and Referrals.

Creating rave reviews is the key to getting your customers to come back to your business—repeatedly. A rave is several steps up from being merely satisfied. A customer who gives you a rave review will, in most cases, become a repeat customer. And repeat customers are usually inclined to tell their friends, family, and coworkers about their wonderful experience with your company, which is the new customer engine of Engagement Marketing.

When you implement the first step of the Engagement Marketing Cycle—Deliver a WOW! Experience—you're strategically creating a steady and sustainable stream of referrals in order to bring new, qualified customers to your business, instead of passively waiting for them to talk about you. It's the perpetual motion machine of small business! The Three Rs create their own energy and keep the wheels of your business turning through the ups and downs of the economy.

GOOD OR BAD, PEOPLE WILL TALK ABOUT YOU

> "More than one in four U.S. consumers read about someone else's bad service experience, and more than seven out of ten who read these posts were influenced to either completely avoid or stop doing business all together with the said company."
>
> —2011 Convergys U.S. Customer Scorecard Research

We've all had both wonderful and downright horrible customer experiences. Whether great or not-so-great, these experiences have one thing in common: People talk about them. And the more extraordinary or outrageous they are, the more people love to tell the story. Let's face it, who doesn't love a good cocktail party anecdote—or, these days, a scathing blog post or negative review? According to the 2011 Convergys U.S. Customer Scorecard Research, the "percentage of U.S. consumers who report a bad service experience is continuing to grow at a rapid pace, climbing 5 percent in 2010 and over 13 percent since 2009." In fact, eight out of ten consumers who have a bad experience will report it to their friends through various channels, including social media.[1] To quote my colleague, Mark Schmulen, "There is no marketing cure for sucking!"

---

[1]http://call-center-services.tmcnet.com/topics/call-center-services/articles/230872-convergys-corporation-research-when-us-consumers-unhappy-theyre.htm.

Consider this example of a "horrible customer experience" story my friend told at a party. She had hired a tree service company to prune her trees. The owner of the company came out to look at the trees and recommended that one of them be removed completely. When my friend asked why, the owner of the company snapped at her, "Where's your husband? I don't like dealing with housewives!" and stomped off. Wow! . . . and not in a good way! My friend was floored by the man's reaction. She later called another tree company; the owner of this company also looked at the tree in question and determined that it had a diseased branch which needed to be removed. He took the time to explain why various trees needed pruning and how he would have his crew proceed with each tree, provided a written estimate, shook her hand when leaving, and did the work on the day specified on the contract. She was positively delighted.

How do you think my friend reacted in response to these two customer experiences? Yep, she told everyone she knew her story, and she called the second tree company again for additional work.

As you can see from this example, your customers remember whether you provide a wonderful or downright awful experience. It's this memory that drives future behavior, according to Matt Wilson, a professor of neurobiology at MIT's Picower Institute for Learning and Memory. In the *TIME* magazine article, "Why Do We Remember Bad Things?"(June 23, 2008), Wilson explained, "We think of memory as a record of our experience. But the idea is not just to store information; it's to store *relevant* information. [The idea is] to use our experience to guide future behavior." In other words, we don't just store our memories—we act on them.

If you want to grow your business, the key is to consistently deliver a great customer experience. This is stating the obvious, but how many customer experiences have you had that you'd rate as "extraordinary"? My guess is that the extraordinary examples happen only rarely, which is a sad state of affairs given that small businesses have such a competitive advantage in this area.

No matter what size your business, you have a limited sales and marketing budget. Ensuring that your best new business comes from existing customers through repeat business and referrals is just plain profitable. First, you spend almost no sales and marketing dollars to get repeat customers to your door. Second, they arrive at your door presold; they already know and trust you. And research shows that repeat customers tend to buy more than new customers, and they tend to be easier to serve because you already know how to work together. So they cost less, spend more, and tell their friends. When those friends show up, they've already been softened by a credible and unbiased review from a raving fan, which makes it much, much easier for you to close the sale. What's not to love?

DELIVER A WOW! EXPERIENCE

"Stash sells high-end funky chic jewelry and accessories. I bought a really cool handmade pearl necklace with a sterling silver skull on it—and it wasn't cheap. One day, I inexplicably lost it. While in the store, I lamented to the owner that it was gone, and she said she would see what she could do to order a new one and would let me know. Four months later—during which I figured she had completely forgotten about me—I got the call: A new necklace was waiting for me. It took so long because the designer had originally done a limited edition, which sold out. Convinced by the store owner to make a new one just for me, she had finally gotten around to it. WOW! I was thrilled. (I found the first necklace soon after—under the couch cushion!)"

—*Melanie DeCarolis*

Do you have a WOW! customer experience? To assess whether you're delivering a great customer experience today, consider what it's like to do business with you from your customers' perspective. Challenge yourself and your team to look at your business practices from the first point of contact to post-purchase service. How do your customers buy? What is their preference for delivery of your product or service? How do they want to communicate with you and how often? If you sell to other companies (versus consumers), how do prospects get their questions answered? What kind of information do they want from you in order to make a purchase decision?

It's easy to fall into a pattern of doing business the way you always have without thinking about why you have certain procedures or practices. As you serve your customers or clients, you make many small decisions about how you conduct your business; and if you have employees, they make these decisions, too (sometimes without your knowledge). Most of these decisions are fine, but I bet that you have areas that could use some fine-tuning—and you may not even know it.

By making your customers the central focus of your business, listening to their preferences and fine-tuning your business model (while making sure you're still making money), your odds of getting that rave review—whether delivered at a networking event or on Facebook, Yelp, or Twitter—go up dramatically.

Delivering a WOW! experience begins by identifying the ways in which people enter your business, including traditional entry points, such as storefronts, offices, phone and e-mail; face-to-face interaction at networking meetings, events, and trade shows; and online destinations, such as your website or blog, Facebook, Google Places pages, or your YouTube channel.

As the business owner, you have the ability to actually test each method of entry. Try calling your business phone number the same way a customer would, for example, to see how you're treated. Are you immediately put on hold for five minutes, stuck listening to a recording that says, "Your call is important to us," every 10 seconds? What happens when you try to access your business website from your smartphone? Can you find important contact information or log in using a drop-down menu? Or is your site built in Flash, rendering it unreadable on Apple devices? When a customer or fan responds to your blog post or tweet—or worse, complains about your customer service or products—does someone from your company respond, or are these comments ignored?

Once you've determined how people enter your business, you'll want to map out how best to deliver a great experience at each entry point. Start with the likely flow at each point of contact depending on your type of business. How will you welcome people, gather information, and answer questions? If your product or service has a long sales cycle or is a considered purchase, how will you help prospects through the decision-making process? If you're a retail business, consider the entire buying process from the minute people walk through your door until they arrive home with their purchases.

As you work your way through each stage of interaction, ask yourself, "What are my customers' objectives? Is there a way for me to deliver a WOW! experience at each stage based on these objectives?" For retail businesses, this WOW! experience could be the actual shopping experience, your return policy, your gift wrapping, or even how you set up your in-store displays (i.e., a less crowded and clean store makes shopping more enjoyable). For a service-based business, your WOW! may be the way you provide quotes or written estimates or the fact that you visit potential clients first in order to learn more about them. The important thing is to find your WOW!—whether big or small—and really fine-tune it.

A key decision about our customer experience at Constant Contact was to answer all customer support calls—fast. Was this hard to achieve and expensive? You bet. It would have been far easier and much less expensive to offer e-mail support only. But it became very clear to us, through talking with our users, that when they create their e-newsletters, events, social campaigns, or surveys, they've set aside 30 minutes and they want to get it done right then. If they have a question or need help, they don't want to send an e-mail and wait an hour (or more!) for a response, they want to talk to somebody now. And while they will use online chat and e-mail, they really prefer to talk to a live person. After years of fine-tuning, we now answer more than 3,000 calls per day with an average wait time of under 90 seconds and the friendliest, most knowledgeable, well-trained team around. Now that's a real WOW!

LITTLE TOUCHES MATTER

"Generations Incorporated is a nonprofit in Boston that places adult literacy tutors in elementary schools and after-school programs. The outcomes for both the kids and the seniors are remarkable: The literacy needle for kids moves significantly forward while the seniors feel a tremendous reward in being able to make a meaningful contribution to their community. Most nonprofits give special attention to the larger donors, which is right, of course. Generations Incorporated, however, always makes me feel like my contributions, no matter how big or small, are important and that I'm an integral part of improving where I live. They do this by e-mailing me regular updates on what they've achieved in the community through donations as well as inviting me and other donors to events."

—*Caroline Shahar*

Don't underestimate the power of "little touches" and the impact they have on people as they interact with your business. Really focus on the entire customer experience from start to finish—including packaging. Mimeo.com, for example, is a company that specializes in printing presentations and reports. Mimeo will ship your documents overnight if necessary so that they arrive at your business meeting, trade show, or office at the time you specify (which is a WOW! by itself). When you receive a package from Mimeo, the outside reads, *"Prepare to be delighted."* It doesn't cost Mimeo anything to add this extra touch to its packaging, yet think about how it makes their customers feel—delighted, I bet!

A simple welcome or hello—whether it happens on the phone, by e-mail, or on your Facebook Page—or thanking someone for leaving a comment or positive review can make a huge difference. No matter what kind of business you have, you can add little touches to show your customers that you care about them. A doctor's office can call you an hour before your appointment to say the doctor is running 30 minutes late. A nonprofit can store your credit card information so that when you attend a fund-raising event, you can quickly register online or over the phone. A consulting firm can send handwritten thank you notes to clients when projects are complete. A manufacturing company can check in after a shipment to make sure everything arrived okay.

Of course, it's always easier to deliver a great customer experience when it's you, the business owner, delivering it directly to the customer. If you have employees, however, you'll have to depend on and trust them to deliver extraordinary experiences. And, in the case of virtual or Web-based businesses, you may have minimal human interaction. In these situations you'll need to work even harder to set yourself up for success.

Empower Employees to Deliver the WOW!

"I love the service I get at the Inn at Weston in Weston, VT. Every time we stay there the innkeepers—Bob and Linda—go out of their way to make it a personal experience, chatting over breakfast (but not too much), ensuring we come for dinner (they have a 4/5 star restaurant onsite), and recalling that we have stayed before."

—*Josh Mendelsohn*

Ensuring that your employees create great customer experiences begins with you, the business owner. You have to make sure that employees know the experience you're trying to create and how customers should feel when they begin and end a transaction with you.

The second step is to hire people who can meet your service goals. During the interview process, you can ask prospective employees to describe the best and worst experiences they've had and how each influenced their desire to return to those businesses, or you can present a customer problem and ask how they would solve it. You'll most likely be able to determine how passionate the individual is about providing extraordinary customer experiences by their answers, but if not, continue to dig until you know whether this person is a good fit for your business.

During the early days of Constant Contact, for example, we hired support staff based upon their technical skills. Over time, we realized that we needed people who enjoyed helping others and explaining marketing and technology. We now hire people who are approachable *and* knowledgeable.

Once you've found a great new employee, you need to reinforce the importance of delighting your customers. It all starts with you: Employees need to see you and their coworkers modeling the customer care experience and then do it themselves.

You'll know you've succeeded when your employees begin sharing ideas with you and their colleagues on how to deliver a better experience.

Listen, Learn, and Adapt

What's the best way to know if you are giving your customers great experiences? Ask for their feedback! Most businesses that we talk to have a good sense of the customer experience through the selling cycle as they spend a lot of time understanding their lead flow, pipeline, and early customer experience. They spend less time thinking about their customers' post-purchase experiences.

Most customers don't speak out if they're mildly dissatisfied or just a little put off by something. This is because we've accepted being treated in just an "okay" way. As the business owner, you probably know when a customer crisis erupts in your business that requires your immediate attention—and that's as it should be. But do you know the minor things that bother your customers? Do you think a mildly bothered client is going to refer a friend? Probably not.

The really good news is that you have lots of easy and inexpensive ways to listen, learn, and adapt to your customers today.

Surveys and Feedback

Make it a point to survey your customers, whether post-purchase, after a project is completed, or annually. Online survey tools are simple to use and really inexpensive. Or give your client a call after a project, or send a paper survey, and ask them to critique your delivery. Beg them to be as harsh as they can be. Consulting company Conversion Rate Experts sends an e-mail survey after every call with hard-hitting questions that include: "What were the three top highlights of the call?" "What is the one thing that you think will benefit you most from this call?" "What were the three worst aspects of the call?" (Ouch!) and "How could we have improved the call?"[2]

You also need to listen to what your customers are saying on the Internet—on blogs, Twitter, Facebook, and review sites such as Yelp. It takes just a few minutes to run searches on each platform to see what people are saying about your company—good or bad. Set up to monitor these channels. Another easy tactic is to set up Google Alerts for your company name. Any time your company is mentioned online, Google will send you an e-mail with a link to the source. And Constant Contact offers NutshellMail, a free monitoring tool that will send you periodic e-mail summaries (you set the schedule) of what people are saying about you across Facebook, Twitter, LinkedIn, and Yelp.

Learn

Now that you have all of this great information, it's time to take action. Feedback is not always easy to hear, and we all tend to explain away that one customer who is unique or troublesome. But less-than-positive feedback is where you will find the insights you need to deliver those great experiences that lead to the Three Rs. Feedback is a gift, so gratefully accept it and learn from it.

Sometimes one of the unexpected gifts of customer feedback is that you'll receive input on additional products or services your customers would like you to provide or other companies with whom you should partner. Keep your ears open—customers often drop real gems that can help you expand your business.

---

[2]Neil Patel, SEOmoz The Daily SEO Blog, October 18, 2011, www.seomoz.org/blog/7-lessons-learned-from-running-a-seo-agency-14225.

Adapt

How does what you've heard from customers impact your business model? What could you change that would make your customers happier or make it easier to do business with you? What one change would your customers really appreciate? Can you afford to make this change and still have a profitable business?

KEEP THE WOW! ALIVE AFTER THE INITIAL TRANSACTION

Delivering a great customer experience will definitely benefit your business, but no matter how great the experience, positive memories fade over time—especially if the actual business transaction was short. To extend the positive associations of doing business with you, it pays to extend the customer experience beyond the point of the actual transaction when possible. In other words, you want to remain top-of-mind with your customers so that they continue to refer you months—or even years—after they've done business with you.

You can use any method to keep in touch, including social media and e-mail newsletters, but the point is, you want to continue to WOW! customers after the initial transaction is complete. A landscaping company, for example, could send its customers an e-mail or booklet in the fall about how to prepare gardens for harsh winters or how to give their yard some TLC when environmental conditions, such as extreme heat or drought, cause stress. A business consulting company can provide its clients with timely tips, either through a monthly e-mail newsletter or by sending links to special white papers or reports. A retail store or day spa can send fashion or skin-care tips and coupons. The point is to make sure that your great customer experience continues beyond the point of transaction.

When we experience something truly exceptional, we want to return to it and/or find a way to stay connected to it. When you deliver a WOW! experience, customers will be interested and open to staying connected with you, which brings us to the next step in the Engagement Marketing Cycle: Entice people to stay in touch.

CHAPTER 3

ENTICE TO STAY IN TOUCH

"Make sure to join our e-mail list for some great specials and news from us!!!"—Request to join In a Pickle Restaurant's e-mail list
—*www.facebook.com/InAPickleRestaurant*

Now that you've delivered a WOW! experience, it's time to encourage customers to stay connected with you. You want to connect so you can build ongoing relationships that, over time, will generate engagement and lead to positive referrals and repeat sales. If you don't make a connection, you're relying on people to remember you and your name, which is a losing proposition.

If you're like me, you sometimes can't remember what you had for dinner last night, let alone the name of the company you did business with six months ago. Case in point: we once hired a branding company to do work for Constant Contact. This company delivered great service and expertise, so I was very happy with them. But they didn't keep in touch with me. Now, eight years later, I've forgotten their name. So even though I've been asked a couple of times if I know a good branding agency, all I can say is, "Yeah, we did work with this great branding company once, but I lost track of them." Opportunity lost.

It's just good business practice to keep in touch with customers and clients. Building these connections is important for two reasons. One, it drives repeat sales. Keeping in touch via e-mail, social media (or even—dare I say it?—direct mail) helps draw people back to your business. And it keeps you top-of-mind. Even if people delete your e-mail newsletter without reading it or only glance at your social post, your name sticks around. They are much more likely to remember you if they need your product or service again and are also more likely to refer their friends and colleagues to you if asked. Out of sight, out of mind. It really is that simple.

"DO I REALLY HAVE TO?"

Small business owners don't like asking for contact information. "I don't want to impose on people" is a concern we hear frequently. Good concern. But if you use the connection to give them great value, it is not an imposition—it's value added. It's an extension of your great experience. In Chapter 4, we will dig into the types of content that will make the connection really, really valuable and engaging so that you (and your team) can feel great about asking customers to connect.

Here's some good news: You're already good at connecting with your customers, especially if you've been in business for a while. Maybe you talk to them on the phone, see them face-to-face when they come into your store, or know their first names and their preferences. If you're a service-based business, you may even know their spouses' names and their golf handicaps.

These personal connections are why small businesses have such an advantage when it comes to Engagement Marketing. But like many small businesses, you may not be making any effort to entice people to connect with you beyond the business transaction. To fire up your Engagement Marketing engine, you have to get comfortable asking people to stay in touch with you—and this has to become an everyday habit. Why? Because you need to capitalize on the power of your great experiences. You need to strike while the iron is hot. The customer or prospect is right in front of you or on your website, blog, or Facebook Page; you need to make the connection before they move on to their busy lives and businesses. How do you get them to connect? You need to entice them.

TELL PEOPLE WHAT THEY'LL GET

"Get Ready to Enhance YOUR Personal Style with Practical Fashion Tips that will Increase Confidence in YOUR Everyday Life with the FREE Total Image Beauty Tool Kit & Nurturing Beauty Style Secrets Publication!"

—Total Image Consultants e-newsletter subscription enticement at www.totalimageconsultants.com

Engagement Marketing is an opt-in marketing method. This means your customers choose whether or not to connect with you. They need to be enticed to make the connection. When you entice people, think about the connection from *their* perspective. In other words, what's the benefit? Why should they bother? What kind of information or offers will they get from you? And how often? If they give you their e-mail address, will they receive a monthly newsletter or weekly special offers? If they subscribe to your blog or join your LinkedIn Group, what kind of content and participation should they expect? Why should they potentially clog up their News Feed by Liking your Facebook Page?

To feel comfortable asking for people's contact information or connection (Like, follow, join, subscribe), it helps to have a solid enticement, such as a preview of your content, and maybe even a reward or offer in return for the connection. Having a great enticement, such as a freebie, white paper, coupons, or special report, goes far in lessening the discomfort you feel in asking people to connect with you. Instead of coming to people "cap in hand" and asking,

"Would you like to sign up for our newsletter?" you can say, "Sign up and get this free report" or "Like us on Facebook and get a coupon good for 20 percent off any item in the store."

How you entice people to connect will depend on your business and what you plan to share with these connections over time. Will you share expertise and advice? "Insider access" to upcoming events and sales? What will make people want to connect with your business? A restaurant could share seasonal menu specials and cooking tips. A professional services firm could share best practices and industry updates. A retail store could alert customers to new products and special sales. The challenge is to find the enticement that gets your customers to say, "Yes, I want to join!"

Ginger Burr, a professional image consultant, makes it very easy for people to connect with her by offering a slew of freebies in her Beauty Tool Kit (Figure 3.1)—everything from a beauty enhancing report and free style guide to an audio interview and an e-course on "detoxifying your wardrobe." Who wouldn't hand over an e-mail address for all of that information?

In the business world, a common approach is to provide information and expertise as enticements to keep in touch. These include analysis of trends, markets, or industries, reports, e-books, white papers, e-newsletters, and the like. Invitations to or special discounts for events, such as tele-classes, webinars, or in-person workshops, are also great enticements. Chris Jaeger, owner of Marketing to Brides Online, and Rick Brewer, principal of Get More Brides, teamed up to offer a free weekly tele-class (Figure 3.2) to photographers, caterers, ministers, bridal shops, and other vendors in the bridal industry.

Accounting Management Solutions offers a free Budgeting Scorecard (Figure 3.3) so you can assess your organization's practices. To get your free report, you have to answer some questions and give your e-mail address.

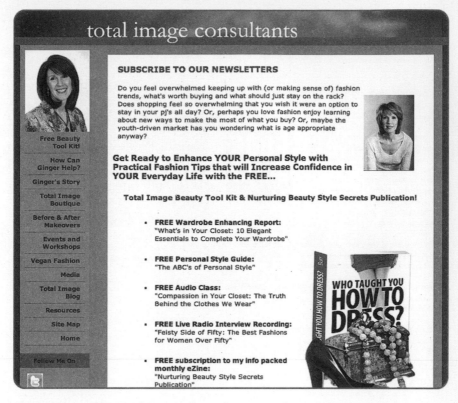

Figure 3.1 The Total Image Consultants newsletter subscription page

On LinkedIn, you can start a Group and offer Group members access to a special website or a free report. HubSpot, an online marketing company, created an Inbound Marketers Group where customers and industry professionals can share information; members have access to additional features at InboundMarketing.com.

Nonprofits can entice donors and volunteers to stay in touch by developing communities where people come to learn, share, and connect, as well as offering e-mail newsletters with news, updates, and special fund-raising events. An animal rescue operation, for example, could post photos or videos of rescued animals, volunteer profiles, and invites to volunteer-only educational events. PSI's

Figure 3.2 Build Your Wedding Business free tele-class sign-up page

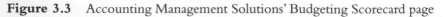

Figure 3.3 Accounting Management Solutions' Budgeting Scorecard page

Figure 3.4   PSI gives people three ways to stay connected

(Populations Services International) home page (Figure 3.4) directs visitors to "Get Involved" and gives three clear routes to do so.

KNOW WHAT YOU WANT (BUT HAVE OTHER OPTIONS)

> "Read our blog. Find us on Facebook. Follow us on Twitter. Learn about our Model Project."
> —*Website calls-to-action for Spa Ni'Joli—http://nijoli.com/*

To begin the enticement process and get people to opt in, you need to be clear about what it is you want from people, whether it's a Facebook Like, a Twitter follow, an e-mail address, or their physical mailing addresses. Too many choices can be confusing, and this can make it hard to build any critical mass. To help build traction, consider funneling people to one or two preferred connection methods. The destination(s) you choose depend on what's working for you already, where your customers are, and the type of business you have.

Spa Ni'Joli, for example, encourages customers and the general public to connect on Facebook, where you can find one-time offers and news (Figure 3.5), but the spa also sends its customers birthday cards with offers in the mail. Both of these tactics help get people back to the spa (repeat sales) and keep the spa top-of-mind for those customers who haven't booked an appointment in a while.

Retail and other types of consumer businesses may simply want an e-mail address and a Facebook Like or a Twitter follow. For businesses selling to people within corporations, a blog, a LinkedIn Group, or an e-newsletter may be the best ways to connect. If you're a nonprofit, you may ask people to subscribe to your e-newsletter and Like your Facebook Page—while your donors get the expanded, full-color print newsletter and invitations to events.

Should you have profiles on all the social media platforms? It's a good idea to create Profiles and/or Business Pages for LinkedIn, Google+, Facebook, and Twitter, but don't worry if you have

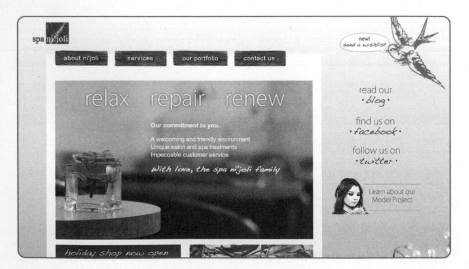

Figure 3.5   Spa Ni'Joli's home page

limited connections on them. Instead, use your less popular connecting points to drive people to your preferred destinations.

To determine which connection methods or destinations are
best for your business, find out what works for your customers.
You have lots of ways to figure this out. You can just ask your customers when they come into your business. To find out if they're
adopting a network like Twitter or Google+ (also called G+),
you could include a survey or poll in your next e-mail, blog
post, or Facebook post. Or you could just test it out and see
if people hop on! Don't assume that your customers are using
a platform just because "everyone else is" or because you're
hearing a lot of buzz. Before choosing a destination, do your
research first! And remember, the landscape of social networking is shifting over time. A few years ago, Twitter didn't
exist and Facebook was for the younger set. As we write this,
Google+ is just getting off the ground. E-mail marketing is a
tried-and-true method for staying in touch that will allow you
to pull people into different social networks over time. I may be
biased here (Constant Contact started in e-mail marketing), but
I think almost every business should have an e-mail opt-in as a
way to connect.

THEY'RE JUST NOT THAT INTO YOU

Although people are more willing to connect with businesses
than ever before, they're also pickier about which businesses they
will connect with. Not everyone will want to stay in touch, and
that is okay. What we've learned at our small business seminars is
this: Roughly one-third of people are passionate joiners of e-mail
lists and social networks and readily engage with companies and
brands. Another third are occasional joiners who tend to watch

versus participate. The final third have a "no way in hell" attitude. They don't want to interact with businesses, they're not tech savvy, or they're not online. As the business owner or marketer, you want to focus on the first group: The people who are passionate about your company and comfortable with putting themselves out there online. The key is not to let the potential "no" deter you from asking and to accept any "no" with a smile. Focus on those people who do want to stay connected to you and build wonderful experiences that will make them happy they've done so.

LET PEOPLE CONNECT INSTANTLY

When you have someone interested, whether online or offline, you need to make it easy and instantaneous for them to take the actions that get them connected to you. When you go into any big store these days, it's almost guaranteed you'll be asked for your e-mail address at the register. Some retailers even offer you a discount coupon right on the spot in exchange for your e-mail address. This is a great way to ask for permission to keep in touch, so it surprises me when small businesses don't make the effort to obtain customers' contact information, especially since they have a real advantage when it comes to building and maintaining deep connections that can last for years.

If you want people to Like your Facebook Page, include your Facebook URL everywhere: on signage, the way Spa Ni'Joli does in Figure 3.6, collateral, business cards, menus, your website, e-mail newsletters, e-mail signatures, and packaging, basically on anything your customers or prospects will see. Heck, I've even seen plumbers and other tradespeople put Facebook URLs on their trucks. And you'll want to train employees to ask people to connect at each transaction. Griswold Dental Associates makes it

Figure 3.6   Sign outside of Spa Ni'Joli enticing people to follow them on Facebook and Twitter to receive notices of last-minute discounts

easy for people to connect with them through e-mail, Facebook, and Twitter by adding these points of connection to their website (Figure 3.7).

If you're collecting e-mail addresses for your e-newsletter or other e-mail promotions, use both high-tech and low-tech ways to collect them. On the high-tech side, you could have iPads or other tablets available and have people sign up immediately, or you could post a QR code that links to your online sign-up form. Some e-mail marketing vendors (including Constant Contact) offer a way for people to join your mailing list via text message. You could subscribe new

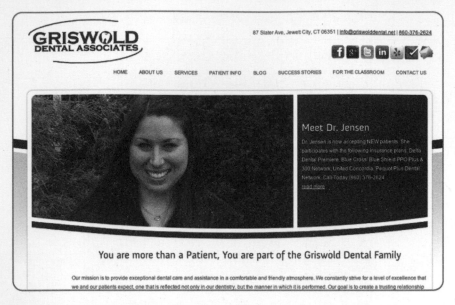

Figure 3.7   Griswold Dental Associates home page

customers yourself on your smartphone. And you should add an e-mail subscription form everywhere customers interact with you online, including your website, shopping cart, blog, Facebook Page, and landing pages for white papers or reports. Figure 3.8 shows how In A Pickle Restaurant added a newsletter subscription form to its Facebook Page. Notice that In A Pickle entices people to subscribe with offers of special deals and discounts.

On the low-tech side, you can put out a good, old paper sign-up book, a fishbowl for business cards, or a special sign-up promotion card for people to fill out. If you attend events to meet prospective customers and collect business cards, you need to follow up and get these folks to opt in to your list. You can start the process by e-mailing them *right after* the event to say something like, "I enjoyed meeting you last night. Since we were talking about XYZ, I thought you might find this issue of my newsletter interesting. I haven't added you to my list (I hate when people do that to me) so feel free to subscribe if you find it of value." You can

Figure 3.8   In A Pickle Restaurant's Facebook newsletter sign-up page

also ask people to connect with you on LinkedIn after the event and include a link to your free report or blog in the invitation.

You want to make sure that you have an easy and immediate way to connect available at every customer touch point.

CLOSE THE PERMISSION LOOP

Permission is perishable. You have only an instant to get it and then the customer is gone. And once you get that permission, you need to use it or lose it. If you collect people's e-mail addresses manually and then upload them two months later (which many small businesses do, unfortunately), people have long forgotten about you, and you've squandered your chance to maintain the connection. Your goal is to close the loop on connecting as quickly as possible.

Once the connection is made, close the loop by welcoming people to your community. If possible, your first communication with your new connections should be a personal welcome versus a "Thank you for joining our community, we look forward to staying in touch" type of response. Warmly greet people as they connect, and don't be afraid to show some personality. People like it when businesses loosen up. You'll want to tailor your Welcome messages to fit the connection type. Below are just a few ideas:

E–Mail List

To ensure that people get immediate value from subscribing to your e-newsletter, include a link to your archived newsletters in your Welcome message or use an auto-responder to send out your three most popular issues. You can also include a link to your online community (blog, Facebook Page or LinkedIn Group) to make people feel welcome and part of the club. Work It Out Fitness (Figure 3.9) gives its subscribers reasons why they should join the fitness club on Facebook and Twitter. Clever!

Facebook

If you have a relatively small Facebook following, greet new people by name as they join, as The White Mountain Hotel & Resort does in Figure 3.10. You can also ask them what they want to see in terms of offers or engagement.

LinkedIn

When people connect with you, thank them for the connection by sending a personal note once the connection is made within the LinkedIn system. If you have a Group, individually welcome new members by name. If it's a popular Group, you may not have the bandwidth to welcome each person individually, but do try to

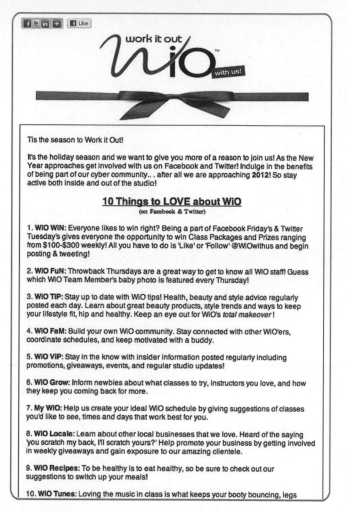

Figure 3.9 Work It Out Fitness e-mail that ties back to Facebook and Twitter

Figure 3.10 The White Mountain Hotel & Resort welcomes new fans on Facebook

make an effort to welcome those who are new. If possible, introduce new people to the "old hands."

Twitter

If you're an active Twitter user and have a large following, it can be a little difficult to welcome each new follower individually. If you have the resources, especially if your follower list is relatively small, it's a nice touch, as you can see in the example of ManGrate Grills welcoming new follower @TheSkrApr (Figure 3.11).

You can also use auto-direct messages (auto-DMs) to welcome people. The general feeling on Twitter, however, is that people find auto-DMs annoying. The only reason you should use them is if you're going to direct people to something of value, such as a free report. Another good way to make use of the auto-DM is to list a few other interesting people your followers may enjoy following. If you're using an auto-DM to say, "Thanks for following" or to send self-serving messages like, "Let's connect on Facebook" or "Read my blog," then don't bother with one.

Blog

If someone new appears at your blog, thank him or her for stopping by and leaving a comment. Blog comments are like gold, so you'll want to make new people feel welcome. For an extra special

Figure 3.11   @ManGrate welcomes a new follower on Twitter

touch, find and follow the person on Twitter or LinkedIn to thank him or her for leaving a comment. Be sure to include a link to the original blog post.

IT'S ABOUT QUALITY, NOT QUANTITY

> "We use Twitter to connect with customers but we make sure we use it to write notes to people or businesses, not just for sending out generic posts. We use the @ symbol a lot."
>
> —*Luke Williams (@truepixfilms)*

Growing your fan base or list is a good objective, but it's not an end in itself. You're better off with a smaller engaged base than hundreds or thousands of people who don't care or don't really remember who you are. The same holds true for your activity level. No one cares if you tweet ten times a day, or even three times a day. You'll get much better traction if you welcome people, care for your community, and post content that engages them, even if you're only posting once a day or a few times a week or sending out an e-newsletter to a few hundred people every month.

Speaking of engagement, this brings us to the next step in the Engagement Marketing Cycle. In the next chapter, you'll learn how to use content to engage people and ultimately draw them back to your business.

CHAPTER 4

ENGAGE PEOPLE

In the last two chapters, you learned how to use WOW! experiences to entice people to keep in touch with you. Now it's time to *engage*! What do we mean when we talk about engagement? We mean reconnecting with people by delivering content that they find interesting and relevant—and, when we hit the target, something that gets them to take an action. These actions can range from very simple to very rich. An action can be as simple as someone reading your blog post and nodding her head in agreement, or as rich as inspiring a customer to share your content with her network or posting a review on Yelp, TripAdvisor, or Amazon to share with friends and colleagues. Engagement also includes everything in between, from Likes, comments, and shares to downloads, event registrations, and online purchases.

Online participation often translates to offline engagement when your customer responds to something you sent out or posted by making an appointment or reservation, stopping by your business, or calling to say, "I've really enjoyed your e-newsletter about what's going on in our industry; I'm ready to talk about how you can help us."

WHY ENGAGEMENT MATTERS

Engagement pulls people back into your business (Figure 4.1) and ultimately leads to repeat sales. And with the power of social media, engagement can drive visibility that brings you new customers. Engagement also reinforces your customers' positive experiences with your business. It makes good on the promise that you made when you enticed people to stay in touch with you.

To engage people—and bring them back to your business—you need a few tools. First, you need content that's worth sharing: news, events, sales, special offers, a poll or survey, breaking news, reports, coupons, and more. Second, you need a call to action that hooks and directs people. Third, you need delivery mechanisms that push your content to your audience: e-mail, social media, RSS, and so on. And fourth, you have to make it easy for people

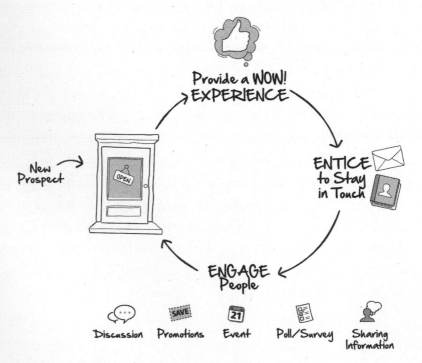

Figure 4.1   The Engagement Marketing Cycle

to interact with you and your content and to share your information with others.

FIVE TYPES OF INTERESTING, RELEVANT, AND ENGAGING CONTENT

Creating engaging content is limited only by your imagination. We've seen small businesses and nonprofits post everything from fun games, customer spotlights, entertaining poll questions, and coupon downloads to thought-leadership blog posts and white papers. Whether your audience is other business owners, consumers, or donors, here are five general types of content to get your creative juices flowing: Question and Answer, Sharing/Information, Discussions, Promotions, News and Announcements, and Events. These can be used separately or in combination.

QUESTION AND ANSWER

If you're just starting out with Engagement Marketing or social media in general, using a Question and Answer (Q & A) format to engage people is a great place to begin. It's easy to create this type of content—and even better, your customers' everyday questions become your source of new content ideas. You can start by answering the questions your customers or prospects frequently ask you. Post the question or scenario, give your initial thoughts, and ask people to add their opinion. You can also incorporate surveys and polls into your Q&A campaigns, a tactic that's very easy to accomplish on Facebook and LinkedIn (both have easy-to-use "widgets" or tools). You can include surveys or polls in your blog posts and in your e-newsletters. In Figure 4.2, Safety Center Incorporated used a poll question to ask its fans what areas of safety concerned them the most.

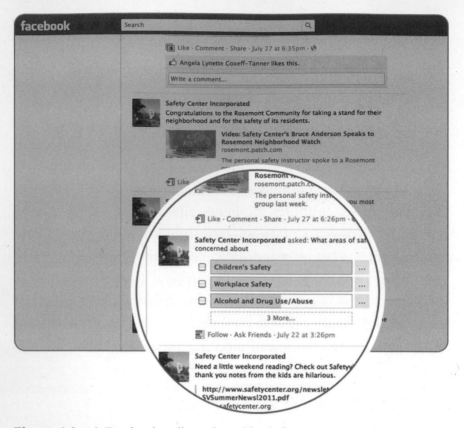

Figure 4.2 A Facebook poll conducted by Safety Center Incorporated

What we love about the Question and Answer format is that if you get good responses to your poll or survey, you can share the results in a follow-up post or in your e-newsletter. If response was really good and you got some exciting data, you can create a special report and promote it using as many channels as possible.

Finally, once you get this started, you will find yourself identifying potential new posts as you go about your business and interact with customers, clients, and prospects. When they ask you a question, make a mental note to answer it online for a wider audience. To source ideas for new content, you can also ask your online connections if they have questions about your products or other relevant topics.

SHARING/INFORMATION

With this type of content, you share knowledge on a topic relevant to your industry or expertise. This can be original content in the form of blog posts, white papers, case studies, infographics, and the like, or sharing other people's content, such as a news item, article, or blog post, and adding your expert analysis or feedback. This is your chance to share your expertise or point of view and build your expert status with your audience.

You can share anything that's new, newsy, or relevant to your audience. In a business setting, this can be content about new developments in your industry, new techniques or practices, client case studies and return on investment (ROI) analysis, or anything you think that will add value to your audience. In today's world, short forms of content are really effective, so there is no need to write pages and pages. You can also focus on curating content from other sources and adding just a little expert commentary, the way Bob Leonard of acSellerant did in a LinkedIn Group (Figure 4.3).

Figure 4.3 Bob Leonard shares a cartoon in a LinkedIn Group

Consumer businesses can post about new products, trends, tips, and techniques, or industry developments. For example, if you own a yoga studio, you might post a yoga pose of the month and share the correct posture and what benefits it delivers. A wine store could feature a wine of the month and food ideas for pairing. A retail shop can post about new merchandise and its benefits or features. All of these businesses can help their customers understand any trending news topics or relevant consumer alerts. In Figure 4.4, Doc Peg Is In shares an article on Facebook.

Nonprofits can share, too. Winter Park Harvest Festival is an annual celebration of the local food scene in Winter Park, Florida. The organization regularly shares news and information about the local food and farming scene. In Figure 4.5, Winter Park Harvest Festival shares a video featuring a tour of an eco-friendly farm. Why is this news "awesome" to its fans? Because its members are passionate about sustainable lifestyles.

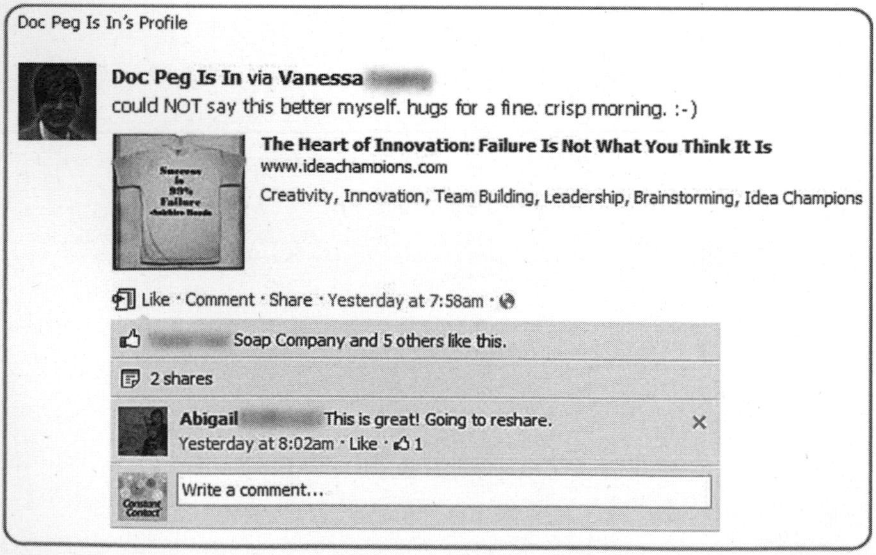

Figure 4.4 Doc Peg Is In shares an article on Facebook

Winter Park Harvest Festival shared a link.
February 29

Check out this cool film about our Urban Farm Manager Tia on her own Econ Farm - filmed by Festival friend Brent - http://t.co/pj6tR2qK

Like · Comment · Share

6 people like this.

Write a comment...

Figure 4.5 Winter Park Harvest Festival shares a video on Facebook

Sharing information and expertise has a number of wonderful benefits for both you and your customers, clients, or members/donors: It showcases your expertise while keeping people abreast of news and happenings; it keeps your company or organization top-of-mind by allowing you to engage with your audience on a regular but informal basis; it strengthens your relationship with past customers or contacts; and it further reinforces positive experiences with your company or organization. You can use your insight, perspective, or analysis to kick off a conversation with your audience. Which leads us to the next type of engagement: Discussions.

DISCUSSIONS

Similar to Sharing/Information type of content, Discussions allow you to present a quick point of view in order to get people engaged in conversation. Think topical, newsworthy, and maybe even controversial. The goal is to draw your audience into a participatory dialogue. The key is to find content that kick-starts the discussion. You can also present your opinion on a topic of interest and ask people if they agree or have a different view. Discussion starters can be as easy as a "fill in the blank" starter. Constant Contact posted one of these simple Facebook discussion starters to our small business audience: "For a small business, change is _____." People jumped in and engaged! Similarly, International Freelancers Day used a "fill-in-the-blank" discussion starter to ask its fans who or what helped them get started in their businesses (Figure 4.6). People loved that question!

You can keep discussions fun and lighthearted in order to encourage people who normally don't engage to add to the conversation. In Figure 4.7, Boloco used a lighthearted conversation starter asking people if they were being lazy or productive on a Sunday to solicit fun engagement.

Kiva, a nonprofit organization, asked its fans to describe the most inspiring gift they had ever received (Figure 4.8).

For companies that sell to other businesses, a discussion kick-starter can include industry news, federal or state legislation, or world events impacting a specific industry. For consumer-related businesses, you can post topics about current events, holidays, or anything that people are talking about. In Figure 4.9, Ginger Burr,

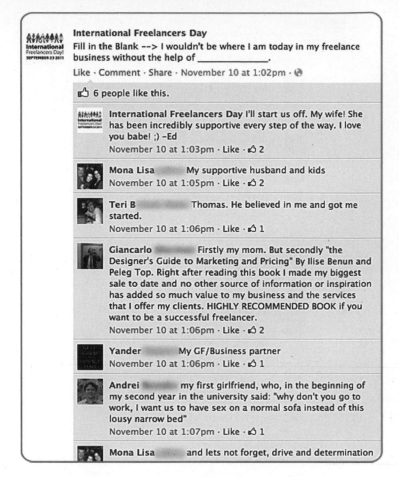

Figure 4.6 International Freelancers Day discussion starter

of Total Image Consultants, takes a stand on boring belts and gets a discussion going with one of her fans.

Discussions can take place on forums, blogs, Facebook, LinkedIn, and, yes, even Twitter. Mack Collier founded BlogChat, which is a live conversation held every Sunday night on Twitter (#blogchat). In Figure 4.10, you can see part of the discussion among @ConversationAge, @LisaPetrilli, and @Ariherzog.

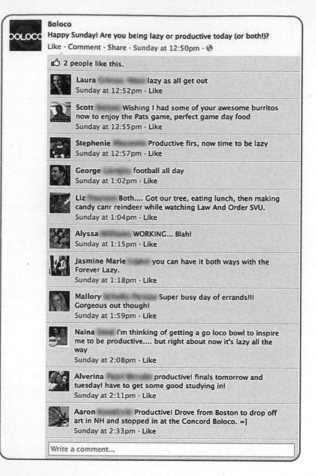

Figure 4.7   Boloco's Facebook conversation starter

To make discussions hum, you should moderate them by commenting back to people and asking follow-up questions to encourage further participation. Some discussions start and end fairly quickly; others can go on for days or more, depending on your platform. Forums and LinkedIn Groups lend themselves to long-term discussions, while Facebook and Twitter posts quickly die out once other news items capture people's attention. When you find a topic that's getting a lot of interest and participation, you should let your audience know and try to stimulate even more discussion. We discuss techniques for restimulation in Chapter 8.

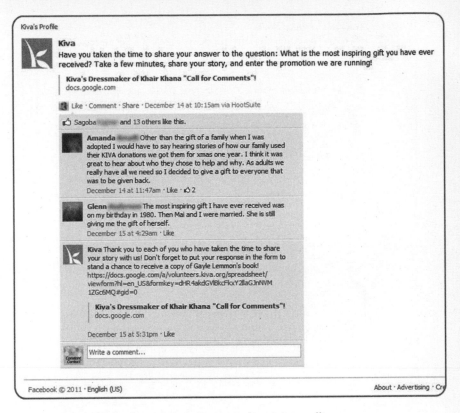

Figure 4.8   Kiva asks a question to get discussion rolling

PROMOTIONS, NEWS, AND ANNOUNCEMENTS

This content type is your opportunity to share offers and company news with your connections. Samples, trial offers, coupons, special sales, e-books, reports, and free consultations are all examples of promotional offers. You can use offers to generate leads via e-mail and direct mail campaigns or to get people back to your physical storefront. In Figure 4.11, Jaffarian Automotive Group offers a discount coupon on an oil change, available to Facebook fans only.

To get people to pay attention to your offer, set a time limit (e.g., "Respond by 5:00 PM today!"), add an expiration date,

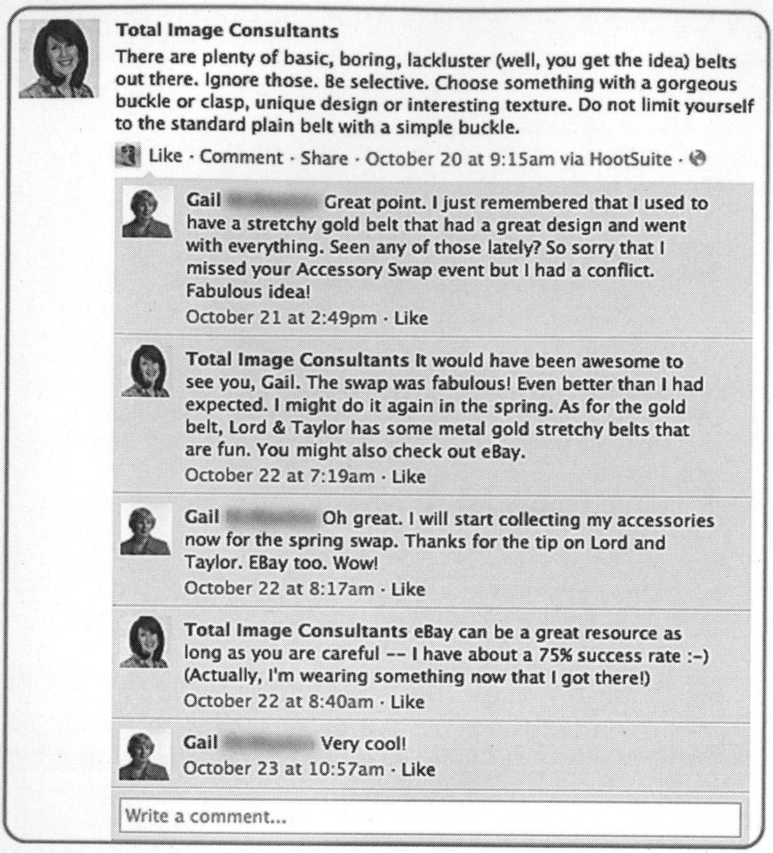

Figure 4.9   Total Image Consultants Facebook discussion

or make it quantity limited. For example, you could state that the offer goes to the first 10 people who post on your Wall or comment on your blog, or you could limit the number of downloads.

Announcements of new products or services or company news fall into this category as well. You should share news that is interesting to your audience. This could include seasonal product availability ("Fall Mums Now in Stock"), changes in your offerings ("New Menu Items Added," "New Services Now Available," or "Extended Holiday Hours"), changes in your team ("Added a

Figure 4.10 #BlogChat Twitter discussion, moderated by Mack Collier[1]

New Tax Partner" or "Welcome to Our New Yoga Instructor") or new offices and locations. These announcements should be focused on the benefits they bring to your connections. Keeping people informed about your business keeps them connected and directs them to products and services that might be of interest.

Figure 4.12 demonstrates how to draw fans' attention to new content on your blog or website by sharing a link on Facebook. On its blog, Learning Ally shared the story of a boy who overcame his reading difficulty to succeed in school. Learning Ally directed

[1]https://twitter.com/#!/BlogchatNews

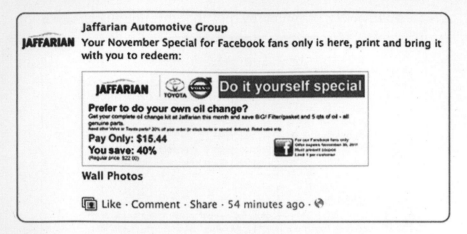

Jaffarian Automotive Group
Your November Special for Facebook fans only is here, print and bring it with you to redeem:

Prefer to do your own oil change?
Get your complete oil change kit at Jaffarian this month and save $6G/ Filter/gasket and 5 qts of oil - all genuine parts.

Pay Only: $15.44
You save: 40%
(Regular price $22.00)

Wall Photos

Like · Comment · Share · 54 minutes ago

Figure 4.11 Jaffarian Automotive Group offers a coupon to its Facebook fans

Learning Ally
Charlie and his mother Liz know what difficulties a learning difference can bring to a relationship, a family and a struggling learner. They also know the experience of turning it all around. Great story on the Learning Ally blog.

Mother–Son Duo on the Challenges of Dyslexia | Learning Ally, formerly Recording for the Blind & Dys
www.learningally.org

"School was horrible. It was frustrating and I never wanted to go. My mom would get emails from teachers saying 'Charlie needs to put forth more effort in his school work.' I tried to explain to everyone that I was doing my best, but no one believed me."

Like · Comment · Share · October 25 at 9:55am

13 people like this.

1 share

Connie If you have a child that struggles with reading, this is an absolutely great website! Your child will experience a whole new world of literacy that works better for them! Check it out!!
October 25 at 10:02am · Like

Saskia wow this story should be sent to every school in the country – teachers should have picked up on this earlier!
October 25 at 6:25pm · Like

Lisa AWESOME story!
October 31 at 8:05pm · Like

Write a comment...

Figure 4.12 Learning Ally shares news of interest to its fans

traffic to this new content by posting the link in a Facebook status. As you can see, this story resonated with Learning Ally's fans—13 Likes, one share, and three comments. This is fantastic engagement! (It's also a great example of making your customers or members the stars of the show, which we will talk about in Chapter 8.)

EVENTS

Events are a fantastic way to engage. In-person events can include workshops or training classes, seminars, user groups or conferences, private sales, parties and open houses, trade shows, sidewalk sales, demonstrations—you name it, you can create it. Constant Contact partners with chambers of commerce to offer free marketing workshops. Kitchen Outfitters, the store where I bought my knives, held a cookbook swap. We all have cookbooks that we don't use, so Willa, the owner of the shop, created this special event where we could trade our cookbooks.

Online events can include webinars and tele-classes, question and answer sessions, demos, guest speakers, and even workshops. Copywriting coach Chris Marlow created a monthlong event where she interviewed 15 successful copywriters. Each interview happened via a tele-clinic (which people could pay to attend), and those on the call could follow up with the interviewee via a Q&A in a LinkedIn Group Chris created (Figure 4.13).

You don't need to do these events alone. If you're part of a retail district in your town or city, you can get together with other businesses to hold a sidewalk sale or educational event. A day spa, for example, could work with local complementary business, such as a wardrobe consultant, to create a "makeover Saturday" or work with a bridal shop for a "Prepare for Your Big Day!" event.

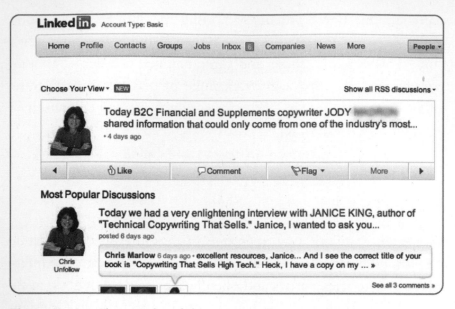

Figure 4.13 Chris Marlow fields questions from copywriters in her LinkedIn Group

For businesses selling to other businesses, seminars or webinars are an excellent way to generate and qualify leads. You can invite people to a "How to . . ." or "Learn about . . ." seminar on topics relevant to your industry. In Figure 4.14, Michael Katz, Principal of Blue Penguin Development, works with small companies and solo professionals. He used e-mail to generate leads via a special webinar titled "Selling Without Selling."

If people register and attend, you know they're qualified. Your current connections can easily pass along event announcements to their colleagues or network.

When your customers or clients attend events, you deepen your connection. And events provide multiple opportunities for social visibility. You can encourage your registrants to share their plans to attend, then get your attendees to post or tweet from the event to drive more visibility for your business.

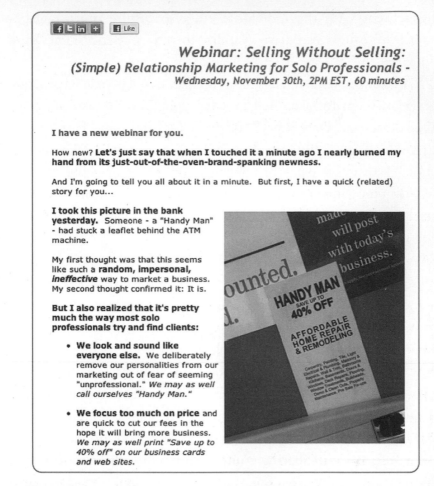

Figure 4.14   E-mail promoting a webinar event from Michael Katz of Blue Penguin Development

CALLS TO ACTION: TELL PEOPLE WHAT TO DO

Social visibility only happens with participation. So, while it's good when people read your content, it's even better if they take some sort of action, such as Liking a post, leaving a comment, or registering for your event. Without a call to action, your content lacks an engagement driver. The best calls to action not only drive engagement with the individual but also inspire more engagement from others and drive visibility to new audiences. Let's look at a successful call to action more closely.

To make your content engaging, you have to tell people what action you want them to take: "Tell us what you think." "Take our poll." "Download our white paper." "Register for our event." Participation has levels: "Read." "Pay attention." "Take an action." "Take another action." Not every piece of content needs to incorporate multiple levels of engagement, of course. What you want to work toward is increasing the level of commitment from people who have connected with you.

For Events, Discussions, Promotions, News, and Announcements, and Question and Answer, the call to action is usually obvious: register for the event, share your thoughts, download (and redeem) the coupon, answer the question, or take the survey/poll. You can add an additional level of participation by asking people to share your content with others who they think might benefit from it, including friends and family, colleagues, and coworkers. You can even incent or reward this sharing. Many of these actions are immediately visible, such as commenting on your Facebook Page or retweeting your offer or announcement.

For Information/Sharing content, different calls to action drive different levels of engagement. Level One is simply "read my content," whether it's a blog post, e-newsletter or tweet. Level Two is "Like or retweet my content." Level Three is "leave comments or feedback." To reach this highest level of engagement, include a link to outside content such as an opinion piece or a news article, then add a "hook" that encourages people to leave a response. Hooks include questions such as "What do you think?" "Do you agree or disagree?" or requests for additional insight such as "Have you experienced this? Share your thoughts." To keep things rolling, moderate the discussion by replying to people's answers as Ginger did in her post about the belts in Figure 4.9.

Your calls-to-action have three major purposes. First is direct engagement with individuals. The more you can get people to participate, the more likely they'll do business with you again in the future. You have reinforced the relationship, added more value, and reminded them about you. Second, participation from one person inspires participation from the next. If someone sees Likes and multiple comments on a post, they're more likely to read the thread and to participate. The third purpose of a call-to-action is that *engagement can drive visibility*. Some calls-to-action, such as sharing, immediately spread your message or content to a wider audience. We will fully examine which calls-to-action drive what types of visibility in Chapter 6.

INVITE EVERYONE TO YOUR PARTY: DISTRIBUTE BROADLY

Once you've created content that's worth sharing and contains a great call-to-action, you need to deliver your content to your audience so that they'll see it and begin the engagement process. You can and should use multiple delivery mechanisms to push your content to your audience regardless of your call-to-action destination. Use whatever channels you have available: e-mail/ e-newsletters, forums, social media, blogs, and your website, to name a few. Many of the tools available to help you promote your content are easy-to-use and low-cost.

For example, if you have a downloadable coupon on Facebook, you can promote it in your e-newsletter, tweet about it, link to it on your website, and, of course, post it to your Facebook Page. If you've sent out an e-newsletter, you can post it to your website and then send people to it via Twitter, Facebook, and LinkedIn. If you've written a blog post, people who have subscribed to it via RSS will see it in their readers; but you can also direct people to the post using Twitter, Facebook, LinkedIn, and e-mail. If you get a few good comments, you can encourage people to add to the discussion through the same multichannel method.

In A Pickle Restaurant used e-mail to alert its customers about a contest for Boston Bruins tickets (Figure 4.15). The restaurant distributed a similar message about the contest to its Facebook fans (Figure 4.16).

You shouldn't blast the same exact message to all channels at the same time. Different networks lend themselves to different techniques, and the timing should be staggered. In Chapter 8, we will cover the techniques for posting across different networks at

Figure 4.15   An e-mail newsletter from In A Pickle Restaurant

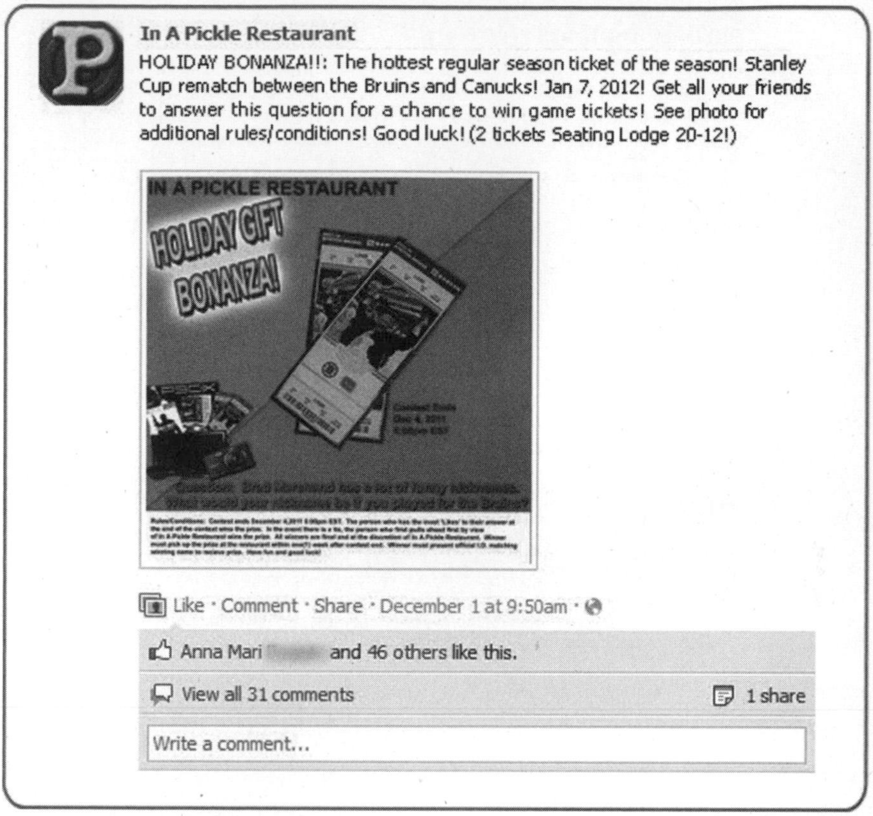

Figure 4.16 The same message distributed to In A Pickle's Facebook fans

different times to drive the biggest visibility for your engagement content.

The key takeaway is that you'll grow your audience—and your engagement—by inviting as many people as possible to view and engage with your content at one destination.

Focus on Quality (Not Quantity) Engagement

When people arrive at your Facebook Page, blog, or Twitter Feed and see others interacting and having fun, they'll want to join, too. The more engagement you have, the more people

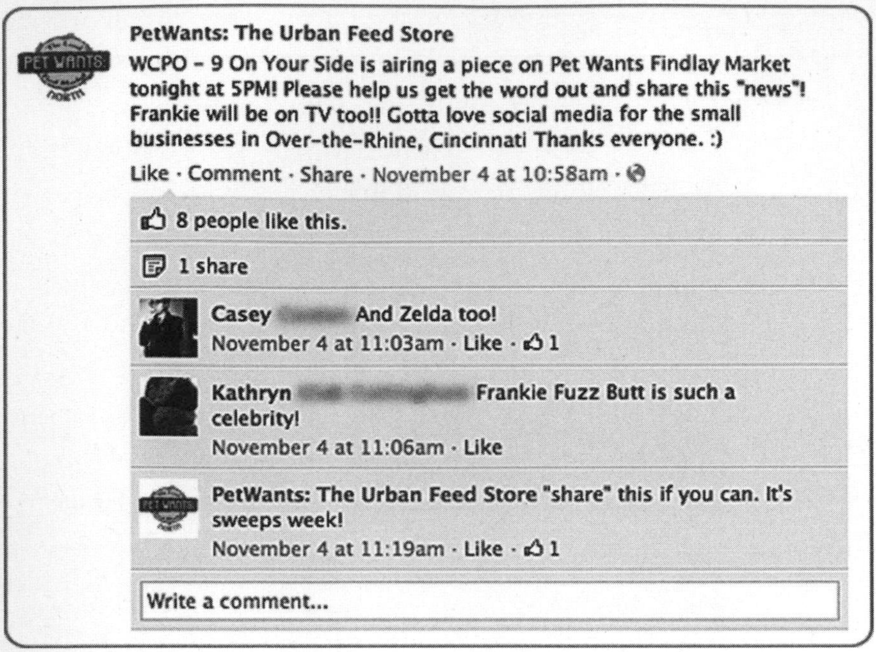
PetWants: The Urban Feed Store
WCPO - 9 On Your Side is airing a piece on Pet Wants Findlay Market tonight at 5PM! Please help us get the word out and share this "news"! Frankie will be on TV too!! Gotta love social media for the small businesses in Over-the-Rhine, Cincinnati Thanks everyone. :)
Like · Comment · Share · November 4 at 10:58am ·
8 people like this.
1 share
Casey And Zelda too!
November 4 at 11:03am · Like · 1
Kathryn Frankie Fuzz Butt is such a celebrity!
November 4 at 11:06am · Like
PetWants: The Urban Feed Store "share" this if you can. It's sweeps week!
November 4 at 11:19am · Like · 1
Write a comment...

Figure 4.17 PetWants shares news with its fans

want to join—and the more other people see this engagement and get pulled in, too. In Figure 4.17, PetWants posted that its store is being featured on a local news station. Eight people Liked the post, one person shared it, and two people left comments. Notice how PetWants linked to Findlay Market, which ensured that its post appeared on Findlay Market's Facebook Wall. Smart!

Having our audience engage with us as they do in the PetWants example is the goal, but building an audience takes time. You'll need to try different content types to find what resonates with your fans. When you're just starting out, view your "small" engagement—the occasional Likes, retweets, and comments—as signs that you're on the right track. While you're building your audience, have fun trying new things. Content, by itself, is "lightweight." By this we mean that it's relatively easy to create a tweet or a LinkedIn or Facebook status update. Try things and see what happens. If something doesn't work, experiment with it or try something else. Engagement Marketing is still very new, and even expert marketers are still feeling their way.

It's also important to know that not everyone will engage with you, which is okay. Some people don't feel comfortable sharing online. And not everyone in your audience is online all the time, which means they'll miss some of your posts. The point of engagement is to show that you're involved and paying attention to what your customers and fans are saying and doing. When people do engage, acknowledge and encourage it. For example, if someone posts a photo of his family eating at your restaurant, you want to respond by gushing over the children and thanking them for coming to your establishment. If you make them feel welcome and cared for, you can bet they'll come back to your establishment, tell their friends by sharing the content you produce in the future, and perhaps even recommend your restaurant on a review site.

What makes Engagement Marketing fun—albeit frustrating, too!—is that you sometimes don't know what will work and what won't. You can post something that you think is relatively simple, and it will catch you by surprise by going viral. Or you spend some time creating content you think is really good, but then the post falls flat. Whether a hit or miss, however, engaging content taken as a whole helps build those solid connections that keep you top-of-mind and return people to your business.

We've now closed the loop on the Engagement Marketing Cycle: Deliver a WOW! experience, entice people to stay in touch with you, and engage people in order to bring them back to your business. Engagement, however, does more than bring your customers back to your business—it also makes your business visible to people who may not have heard of you. In the next two chapters, we'll show you the real magic of Engagement Marketing: *Social visibility that drives new prospects to your door.*

CHAPTER 5

How Engagement Marketing Drives New Prospects to Your Door

Engagement Marketing is a powerful way to drive new business. When you get your Engagement Marketing cycle humming, your current customers, clients, and fans will engage in ways that are socially visible, which you can see in Figure 5.1. That social visibility is gold. When people see their friends and colleagues engaging with your business on Twitter or Facebook, that social activity puts your business on their radar with a referral thumbs-up. Social visibility uses the social networks of your current customers to expand your market reach.

Socially visible engagement also provides a big boost to all of your other sales and marketing efforts. Likes, comments, and reviews are visible to new prospects and add third-party customer credibility to your sales pitch. Increasingly, search engines and the social networks themselves are using engagement data to rank search results. So the more engagement you generate, the more likely you are to be found by the next person searching for what you have to offer. In this chapter, we'll explain how social visibility drives new business. Then, in Chapter 6, we'll examine how social visibility happens across each network.

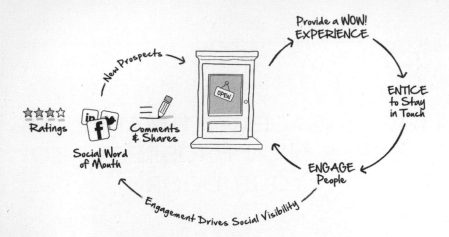

Figure 5.1 Engagement Marketing drives social visibility

ENGAGEMENT DRIVES SOCIAL VISIBILITY

All engagement is good. Most engagement happens between you and an individual client or customer. When you write a piece of content (newsletter, blog post, Facebook post, and so on), most of your audience will read it, maybe smile, nod their heads, and even follow a call-to-action like registering for the event or downloading your white paper. This is one-to-one engagement—and it's fantastic.

In our new digitally connected community, some user actions are visible to the world. Those actions are even more valuable than one-to-one engagement. When people Like, comment, tag, forward, retweet, or share your content, they are not just engaging with you, they are showing that engagement to the world and, in many cases, distributing your content. This is what's known as social visibility.

When your business becomes socially visible, some terrific things start to happen. As engagement begins to build, references to your business begin popping up in the social media sphere.

Your engaged customers mention you in discussions. They review and rate you on the various directory and review sites. These discussion streams and reviews have the potential to be seen by all of the conversation's participants as well as their entire networks—including people who haven't heard of your business. When you consider that the average Facebook user has 120 friends,[1] you quickly realize how many people can be reached with just one share. When these prospects see you engaging with your fans, their confidence in you goes up, which in turn predisposes them to do business with you. As more people engage and your social visibility grows, it becomes easier for new people to find you in the search engines, sending still more people to your door. Social visibility is a win-win-win—for you, your customers and clients, and your prospects.

PEOPLE LEARN ABOUT YOUR BUSINESS

Social visibility's biggest benefit is that it allows people to learn about your business. Let's say you're a shop that sells specialty birding supplies and you're offering a free in-store class on how to identify and attract birds to backyard feeders. You can post a flyer at your cash register, but only the customers who come into the shop will see it. You can also post your event on your Facebook Page. Your customers, Bob, Sue, and Ann, see this post and excitedly let their social networks know that they're planning to attend by sharing your post. This action means that their friends, some of whom are fellow birders, learn about your business. By sharing your event with their well-qualified networks, Bob, Sue, and Ann have exposed your business to new people who may not have known you existed.

---

[1]Facebook, 2009, www.facebook.com/note.php?note_id=55257228858.

What's even better is that social network sharing is targeted, meaning that Facebook and Twitter deliver news about your business to people who are likely to find it relevant. We've all become very good at scanning our e-mail and social Feeds for information that's relevant to us. If Bob's friend and fellow birder Steve sees Bob's share in his Facebook Feed, he's going to pay attention to the post because it's relevant to him. Because it's relevant, he may click on the link, visit, and even Like your Page giving you the opportunity to engage with him and potentially his network. Bob's share did more than just reach Steve about your store but also let Steve know that Bob knows and trusts your business.

WHEN PEOPLE ENGAGE, THEY ALSO ENDORSE

We pay attention to what others are doing and look to our networks for input on businesses, products, and services. Our networks act as our guides by helping us cut through clutter and make decisions about the content we see. Let's say Joe and his friend, Peter, share a passion for fine French cuisine. If Joe eats at your new French restaurant and shares his WOW! experience with his network (which includes Peter), Peter is now predisposed to try your restaurant, too. "Hmmmm, if Joe liked it, it must be good," Peter thinks, and maybe he picks up the phone to make a reservation.

This type of influential behavior is based on a concept called "social proof." Also known as "informational social influence," social proof is defined by Wikipedia as "a psychological phenomenon where people assume the actions of others reflect the correct behavior for a given situation." The concept of social proof explains why Peter, in the example above, is now predisposed to have dinner at your restaurant after reading about Joe's experience.

Aileen Lee, a partner at venture firm Kleiner Perkins Caufield & Byers, posits that "social proof is a relatively untapped gold mine in the age of the social Web."[2] She goes on to list five types of social proof: Expert, Celebrity, User, Wisdom of the Crowds, and Wisdom of Your Friends. This last, says Lee, is the "killer app in terms of one-to-one impact and the potential to grow virally."

Social proof combines our connection to others in our group with the power of endorsement. When Joe eats at your restaurant and tells his friends about it on Facebook, Twitter, or Google+, two factors are at work: first, he's bragging a bit because he's found this great new restaurant and he wants his friends, who also enjoy good food and new restaurants, to know he ate there; and second, he's giving you an endorsement (albeit an implied one). The very fact that we mention, call out, or engage with a business implies that we like this business, because generally speaking, we don't engage with businesses we don't like (at least not in a positive way). Maybe Joe's friend Peter makes a dinner reservation or maybe he doesn't, but with the increased exposure—and Joe's implied endorsement—come trust and relevance that you just can't buy through traditional advertising.

Social proof works the same way for companies that sell to other businesses, too. Susan and Mary are PR professionals who used to work together and are now connected on both LinkedIn and Twitter. When Susan attends your PR firm's webinar and tweets about the content, Mary is alerted to both the expert content and your firm. She's likely to follow your firm on Twitter, subscribe to your blog, and maybe even sign up for the next webinar. That's the power of socially visible engagement with its implied endorsement.

---

[2]"Social Proof Is the New Marketing," *TechCrunch*, November 27, 2011.

Engagement goes beyond just implied endorsements. Engagement can inspire people to leave a positive comment or review or recommend your business. This is explicit endorsement. Explicit endorsements tip the balance in getting people to do business with you. Explicit endorsements can be found on review sites such as TripAdvisor or Yelp, social platforms LinkedIn, Facebook, and Twitter, and search engine, such as Google Places. They can also be found on your website in the form of testimonials and case studies.

Explicit endorsements are important for two reasons. One: when you run a search on a review site such as TripAdvisor, those businesses with the most favorable rankings appear first. Two: endorsements carry social proof. If 50 people think your business is awesome, these endorsements make it really, really easy for someone new to do business with you without having to think about it.

We trust our networks. What's relevant to our friends, family, and coworkers is relevant to us as well. By building your business's social visibility, you garner free visibility to a well-qualified audience—the social networks of your customers—while building trust with people who haven't yet done business with you.

Engagement Enhances All Other Marketing

A well-humming Engagement Marketing engine has another benefit as well: online engagement allows people to get to know you before they do business with you. Socially visible interaction gives prospects a way to see what your clients and customers are saying. Ever visited a company's Facebook Page only to find the last post was made months ago? And they only have three fans? What kind of an impression do you think that makes? An active social presence tells prospects you're running an engaged business, and they can get an immediate sense of your customers' feelings about the business. When prospective customers and clients watch you engage with your existing customers, they can see all of the positive comments and they can see if you respond to people's concerns and questions. They can also see whether your content is valuable or self-serving. When they visit your profile, they can see the comments, shares, and recommendations people leave.

Most important, they can see how you handle negative comments. Yes, you may get someone who didn't have a WOW! experience with your business and this person says something negative. Don't be afraid of negative comments, because they give you a great opportunity to turn a situation around. Often, people who leave negative comments become your biggest fans when they find that you're willing to resolve their issues or concerns. Best of all, your prospective clients and customers see this interaction and learn that you are responsive.

This kind of visibility adds social endorsement fuel to all of your current sales and marketing efforts. Engagement Marketing is not a replacement for your current sales and marketing activities. Rather, it's an enhancement. Engagement is the social proof point for people who find you in other ways, including pay-per-click, search, word-of-mouth referrals, PR, and advertising. When they reach your social media page and see engagement in the form of Likes, comments, shares, and reviews, they get the social proof that increases their confidence and interest.

Engagement Marketing Nurtures Prospects, Too

Prospects can use a social connection as a way to start getting to know you. By Liking your Page, subscribing to your newsletter, adding you to a Google+ Circle, connecting with you on LinkedIn, or following you on Twitter, people are essentially saying they want to learn more about you. Over time, as you deliver engaging content and they see others engage with you, they begin to build trust in you and your company. This trust makes them primed to do business with you when they're ready.

When people engage, they qualify themselves. If I'm not interested in a company's products or services, I'm not going to spend time engaging with them—ergo, I'm not a good prospect. Through the act of engagement, a prospect raises her hand. "Yes, I'm interested in your company," she's saying. "I may need your services. Help me get to know you a little more." Engagement Marketing makes every marketing dollar you spend more valuable. People who have engaged with you become customers at higher rates, and they in turn tell their friends about you, starting the cycle again.

SOCIAL BOOSTS SEARCH RELEVANCE!

Google and Bing/Yahoo! are increasingly relying on social media signals to provide fresh search results. Google, especially, is shifting its algorithms toward news and results that are happening right now rather than serving up links to older content. The search engine now includes data from its own Google+ network (this means that having a profile and/or Google+ Business Page is important) and real-time data. In addition, each search engine provides social media profiles and reviews in its search results. A socially savvy business can often "own" the first page of Google or Bing/Yahoo! for its business name due to having a wealth of content, including website pages, blog posts, press releases, social media profiles and business pages, reviews, and videos.

The search engines take these social media signals seriously and reward socially savvy companies by pushing their sites higher for keyword searches. These searches have the potential to draw new people to your business and push less savvy competitors down in the search results. In addition, more and more sites now show people if someone in their network has shared, Liked, Tweeted, or 1+'d the content on Facebook, Twitter, or Google+. Social engagement will increasingly influence where and how your company shows up on the search engines and social networks. That's one more way your Engagement Marketing will drive new customers and prospects to your door.

While all engagement is good, some engagement actions are more socially visible than others. In the next chapter we'll show you the socially visible calls-to-action that lead to increased engagement—and new business—and give you tips on how to inspire people to use them.

PART II

GET MORE BUSINESS WITH ENGAGEMENT MARKETING

CHAPTER 6

HOW SOCIAL VISIBILITY HAPPENS

Having your customers opt in to keep in touch with you is great. Having them Like, +1, or comment on your content is even better. Having these customers share your content with their social networks is marketing gold.

Sharing content is the heart of the new prospect engine of Engagement Marketing. People who don't know about your business see the content that their family, friends, and colleagues share online—and these interactions carry explicit or implied endorsements. When customers share your posts, you gain exposure to a whole new audience through social visibility. Because these shares link directly back to your social presence, your new audience can easily click through and learn more about you. These people are your new prospects! You now have an opportunity to convert them, because when they visit your Page, website, or blog, they can see your customer engagement and can choose to Like, follow, or opt in to receive messages from you.

Remember, the Engagement Marketing engine consists of three things: provide a great experience, entice customers to stay in touch, and engage people. Once someone has opted in to receive messages from you, the stage is set for you to turn this person into a fan, and ideally a repeat customer, and then the cycle starts all over again. So how do you get people to share? First, it helps to understand that different activities drive different levels of social visibility. This visibility begins with the type of content you create (sharing/information, question and answer, events, and so on) and the respective calls-to-action that drive customer engagement. When people tweet about your business, share your content, link to you, comment on your posts, or leave reviews or recommendations, other people see this activity, either in their News Feeds or on their friends' Walls/profiles. To make your content socially visible, you have to understand how it moves beyond your fans' Walls and profiles and into the Feeds of their friends.

In this chapter, we demystify the sharing process and show you how the different social platforms can spread the word about your business. You'll learn which activities significantly impact social visibility as well as when and how to ask for a share.

SOCIAL VISIBILITY BY PLATFORM

Each social network (such as Facebook, Twitter, LinkedIn, and Google+) works a little differently. It helps to understand the most frequent activities on each platform and where they are visible. To help you see how content moves through the social sphere, we've included charts and screen shots of the major engagement activities for each platform. To keep things simple, we've included only "organic" or user-initiated activities and have left out the paid advertising programs that each platform offers.

Social media networks are frequently changing the actions that people can take and the visibility and impact of those actions. They tweak and tune to find the best formula to make their platforms engaging and useful. They add things and take things away. Odds are that some of the actions we describe here might have changed by the time you read this. That's okay. Use this chapter as a guide, but focus on understanding the concepts and becoming adept at observing the social visibility dynamics of each platform. Once you get the idea, you'll suddenly start noticing what you see in your own personal accounts—and what you don't. To keep abreast of social media changes, review our comprehensive list of publications, tools, and other resources in Chapter 10. You can also visit Constant Contact's Social Media Quickstarter at www.socialquickstarter.com to learn more about each platform. To help you get the most out of your Engagement Marketing efforts, you'll find detailed tips and tricks in Chapter 8 and advice for overcoming common obstacles in Chapter 9.

In the following section, we cover social visibility with regard to the four major platforms: Facebook, Twitter, LinkedIn, and Google+.

FACEBOOK

With over 800 million active users[1] and counting, Facebook is the preferred destination of choice for many consumer-related businesses and nonprofit organizations. Facebook is also becoming much more important to companies that sell to other businesses. A relatively new feature, Timeline (which replaces the Wall for personal profiles) graphically displays what we Like, listen to, read, and watch for all of our friends to see. Timeline allows people to create graphic profiles that include all interests, such as favorite restaurants, movies, spas, books, hobbies, and more. Hence, engagement becomes even more crucial to businesses. As this book was going to press, Facebook announced that as of March 30, 2012,

---

[1]Facebook, December 2011, http://newsroom.fb.com/content/default.aspx?NewsAreaId=22.

all Pages would be transitioned to the Timeline, featuring a new design and functionality.[2]

Facebook is inherently an opt-in platform. Aside from ads, your News Feed only contains information from people, companies, or groups you have connected with (added as a friend, Liked, subscribed, or joined). Increasingly, Facebook interaction unfolds through the News Feed, so getting into the News Feed is a great way to get visibility. When a customer or client Likes you, your content will show up in his or her News Feed immediately after it is posted.

When customer Jane Smith interacts with your posts or writes on your Wall, that activity shows up on her Timeline. If Jane's friends or colleagues visit her Timeline directly, they will see her interactions with you, creating a bread crumb trail directly back to your business. That's good. Even better is when your customers take actions that not only appear on their own Timelines but also get broadcast into the News Feeds of their friends. To keep the sequence straight, think about content moving this way:

Your Business Page → Your Customers' (Fans) Feeds → Their Friends' Feeds

This second degree of separation is what marketers mean by the term "viral."

A number of factors come into play in determining where a story appears in your News Feed. Stories from people you've marked as "close friends" appear at the top, usually as highlighted stories. Stories that have a lot of engagement in the form of Likes and comments also appear at the top of your News Feed. And if you engage with a person (Facebook profile) or a business or organization (Facebook Page), their stories will appear at the top of your Feed (for a while).

---

[2]Facebook.com/help.

Figure 6.1 is a representative sample of which Facebook activities show on your customers' Timelines, in their Tickers, and in their friends' News Feeds. (The Ticker is Facebook's "real-time" Feed. Your friends can see the posts, comments, and Likes that you share with them in their Tickers. However, not everyone has a Ticker as this feature appears only if you have a certain level of activity on Facebook.[3]) As you can see in the chart, most engagement activities appear on your customers' Timelines and Tickers. These are visible to their friends if they visit your fans' Timelines.

Facebook

Action	Appears on Followers' Walls	Appears on Followers' Walls/Timelines	Appears in Feeds of Friends
Like the Page	Appears under "Most Recent Activity"	Yes	No
Like a Post	Ditto	Yes	No
Like a Comment	Ditto	Yes	No
Leave a Comment on a Post	Ditto	Yes	No
Share a Post/ Share an Image/ Share a Link to a Page	Ditto	Yes	Yes
Leave a Post on Page Wall	Ditto	Yes	No
Check in (Location)	Ditto	Yes	Yes
Check in and Tag Friends	Ditto	Yes	Yes
Leave a Recommendation on Page	Yes–If Person Chooses "Public, Friends or Custom"	Yes	No

Figure 6.1   Socially visible Facebook Activity

---
[3] www.facebook.com/help/ticker.

As this book was being finalized, Facebook was making modifications to some of its features, which may impact what shows up in the News Feed. It appears that the changes will enable users to take actions to increase their chances of begin seen in the News Feed. At the same time, individual users will be able to adjust what types of posts they see from their friends. So, regardless of what actions are taken to increase News Feed visibility, what is actually *seen* in the News Feed will depend on both individual users' settings and how Facebook serves up content.

Facebook has four actions that you can use to help move your content into the News Feed of your fans' friends. Shares are the most common and most powerful way to make this happen.

Each piece of content you post on your Page has a built-in "share" function, making it very easy for people to share your content with their social network. When Sue shares your content, Sue's friends see this share in their Feeds. With the share action, your customer can add comments. Facebook also posts the original content with pictures and links, making it a very rich listing in the News Feed. As you can see in Figure 6.2, Donna's Gourmet Cookies posted pictures of its holiday cookies. That posting was then shared by one of the company's fans, Ilene Ross, with a comment (as you can see in Figure 6.3)—which meant that her friends saw it as well! Ilene's comment is just the kind of informal endorsement we all hope to get for our businesses.

BUSINESS CHECK-INS/TAG A FRIEND

Other socially visible actions include check-ins and tagging people. When someone checks in to your business, as Michael did in Figure 6.4, his action appears in his friends' Feeds. When Michael checked in to Training Effects, he also tagged the person he was

Figure 6.2 Original post from Donna's Gourmet Cookies

with—which means Joe's friends will also see the check-in. A check-in has one other huge benefit: It includes a link back to your Page. In Figure 6.4, Training Effects is hyperlinked, making it very easy for people who don't know about the business to visit its Page and learn more about it.

Businesses that want to increase traffic, bookings, or appointments can use check-ins effectively. Restaurants, bars, small shops, yoga studios, hair salons, day spas, and gyms can all use check-ins. You can use incentives to encourage people to check in. If you're a restaurant, for example, you can offer a free drink or special (e.g., "It's Taco Tuesday! Check in and get 75¢ tacos!"). You can promote your incentive on Facebook, on signs in your location, and on any of your collateral (such as menus or table cards).

Figure 6.3   Ilene's share with a comment as it appeared in her friends' Feeds

TAG A PHOTO

You can tag photos on your Page in one of two ways.

First, you can post photos of your customers or members to your Page and ask people to tag themselves. This action can get your photo—and a link to your site—into your fans' friends' Feeds. (We explain how this works more fully in Chapter 8.)

Second, if you're the Page Administrator, you have a personal Facebook profile, and you happen to be friends with the customer(s) in question, you can tag them in your Page's photos. In other words, you cannot tag someone in photos that are on

Figure 6.4 Michael's check-in to Training Effects

your Facebook Business Pages unless the person tagged is a friend in your personal network.

For example, Callie Durbrow is the owner (and Page Administrator) of Durbrow Performance Personal Training. In Figure 6.5, she posted a photo to her business Page and tagged the people who are already her friends on her personal profile. This type of tagging also gets your photo into the News Feeds of the friends of the people who are your business's or organization's fans.

Featuring photos of your customers is a great way to showcase your business, provide engaging and credible content, and gain great social visibility.

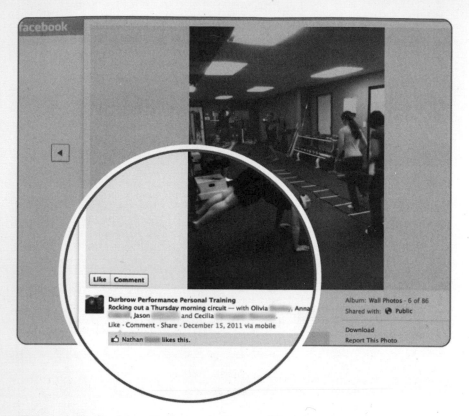

Figure 6.5   Durbrow Performance Personal Training photo tag

PARTICIPATING IN SURVEYS/POLLS

Surveys and polls are great ways to get people engaged, and they're easy to create using Facebook's built-in app. When Joe participates in your poll, this action shows up in the Feeds of Joe's friends, encouraging more people to take your poll. Polls also include a link that allows people to follow the poll results. The poll, of course, links back to your Page—driving new people to your business.

As you can see, Facebook is a social platform that's rich in activity and opportunity. The activities listed above are just a few of the basic things that you can do to keep in touch with customers and reach prospects. To learn how to use more advanced tactics and to keep up-to-date with Facebook's changes, be sure to check socialquickstarter.com on a regular basis.

TWITTER

Twitter is very different from Facebook. For one thing, it's a very public platform. Additionally, it's more of a broadcast channel. Almost all content on Twitter is publicly visible. Twitter allows individuals and businesses to post content or "tweet" (update their status) using 140 characters or less. Anyone can read your tweets without having to follow you (assuming they find your profile). Most people either read tweets in their Feed (tweets from people or groups they follow) or read tweets based upon hashtags and/or keywords (that's how you follow a topic, event, or interest area).

When your customers, clients, or prospects follow you, your tweets appear in their Twitter Feed. If they like your content, they can send it on to their followers by retweeting (RT), which immediately extends your reach. Think of retweeting as "forwarding a message to others." They can also mention (e.g., @mention) you in their tweets using your Twitter handle; the @mention is a clickable link back to your profile. This is why it's important to include a link to your website or blog on your profile, as @mentions and retweets provide the bread crumb trail back to your business.

As on Facebook, some of the engagement activities, including @mentions, RTs, and sharing links, are more socially visible than others, as seen in Figure 6.6.

You can also choose which e-mail notifications you receive about activities happening on your Facebook and Twitter Feeds. Likewise, when you take a social action (comment on a Facebook post, retweet, tag someone in a photo on Facebook,

Twitter

Action	Appears on Profile	Appears in Followers' Feeds
@ Mention	Yes	Yes
RT	Yes	Yes
Share a Link	Yes	Yes
Post a Photo	Yes	No
Add Someone to a List	No (Appears in the list which is on the profile)	No
Follow Someone	Yes	No
"Favorite" a Post	Yes	No

Figure 6.6   Socially visible Twitter activity

follow someone new on Twitter, etc.), there's a good chance there will be an e-mail notification about your action in someone else's e-mail box.

When Joe @mentions you in a tweet, retweets your tweet (or a post that includes an @mention of you), or shares a link to your content, these actions appear in the Feeds of everyone who follows him. One thing to note: If you begin a tweet with "@name," (e.g., @gail_goodman) only people who follow both you and that person/brand will see it. Starting a tweet with an @mention is like sending a semi-private message. If you begin a tweet with commentary, *then* add the @mention, all your followers will see it. All tweets, with the exception of direct messages or DMs, are visible on your profile.

In Figure 6.7, Anita Campbell, CEO and publisher of *Small Business Trends,* has used the @mention tag to call out individuals. She has also linked to and retweeted some interesting content.

A tweet can be retweeted and shared hundreds or even thousands of times. Even better, a tweet can include a link to your

Figure 6.7   *Small Business Trends'* Anita Campbell's Twitter Feed

content, an @mention of your business, and a retweet—all at the same time—extending your reach far beyond your social circle. Tweets can also include links to anything that's online: blog posts, Facebook or Google+ posts, web pages, images, videos, PDFs, and more.

You can use a few tools and tricks to encourage people to share your content on Twitter. If you have a blog, include Twitter's retweet button on your posts. And instead of simply tweeting your blog post headline, think of something that will capture people's attention and get passed around. If you archive your e-newsletters online, include a Twitter "share" button in each archived issue. If you're doing a survey and want to get the word out, ask your network to retweet your post. And, of course, create engaging content that people will want to share!

LINKEDIN

Often referred to as the "B-to-B" or business-to-business social networking site, LinkedIn allows you to post the equivalent of an online résumé and connect with other professionals in your industry—along with a whole bunch of other activities. LinkedIn has personal profiles, Groups, and Company Pages. We will discuss each of these separately. LinkedIn is all about seeing the activity of the people you're connected to or "LinkedIn" with. Your connections are your network. The nice thing about LinkedIn is that anything you do (answer a question, update your reading list, etc.) is visible to your network, provided that the activity Feed is turned on. These actions appear in the Feeds of your connections, as seen in Figure 6.8.

LinkedIn is all about networking and exchanging information—especially relevant and engaging content in the form of reports, e-books, webinars, and polls/surveys, which you can create using LinkedIn's widget. To get your content into the Feeds of your connections—and their connections, too—link to it in your status updates. Similar to Facebook, status updates include a "share" button, making it easy for people to share your content.

You can also share tweets directly to LinkedIn by joining your Twitter and LinkedIn accounts. You can choose to share every tweet to LinkedIn, or you can choose to share only tweets that contain the "#in" or "#li" hashtag. When promoting your content, it pays to post it on Twitter, as well. Many people do link their Twitter and LinkedIn profiles; if they retweet your tweet, it will appear in their LinkedIn status update and on their connections' Feeds, as well.

As you can see in Figure 6.9, Joe Pulizzi of the Content Marketing Institute posted a link to a report on content marketing lessons learned in 2011. This update appeared in the Feeds of his 500+ connections. One of his connections shared the report, which was picked up by Jan O'Daniel, who shared it with her

LinkedIn

Action	Appears on Profile	Appears on Connections' Feeds
Update Status	Yes	Yes
Comment on Status	Yes	Yes
Share a News Story	Yes	Yes
Add Apps to Profile (Blog, TripIt, etc.)	Yes	Yes
Recommend Someone	Yes	Yes
Get a Recommendation	Yes	Yes
Connect with Someone	Yes	Yes
Update the Apps (i.e., Add a Book to your Reading List)	Yes	Yes
Post a Question/ Answer a Question	Yes	Yes
Update Your Profile	Yes	Yes
Join a Group	Yes	Yes
Post a Group Question	Yes	Yes
Answer a Group Question	Yes	Yes
Like a Post Within a Group	Yes	Yes
Create a Poll	Yes	Yes
Follow a Company	Yes	Yes

Figure 6.8 Socially visible LinkedIn activity

500+ connections (Figure 6.10). You can see how Joe is getting great social visibility and distribution through LinkedIn sharing! When content is shared across LinkedIn and gains traction, it can also appear on the network's news page, LinkedIn Today.

LinkedIn Groups

Another way to share information is through LinkedIn Groups. Groups function similar to forums or discussion boards: Someone

Figure 6.9   Joe Pulizzi shares content with his connections

posts a question or observation and then asks Group members for their insights, answers, or feedback. LinkedIn Groups are a great place to get feedback on content you're in the process of creating, test new ideas, get questions answered, or post your survey or poll. You can also post links to your own high-value content, as long as it's not self-serving. (Many Groups are moderated; Group Managers have the power to delete anything that looks, smells, or feels like spam.)

When you link to your content within a Group as a means of starting a discussion, all members within the Group can potentially see it and comment on it—and these comments appear in their connections' feeds. If your content is especially thought-provoking (or maybe a little controversial!) discussions can run for days or even

Figure 6.10   Jan O'Daniel shares Joe Pulizzi's content

weeks. Each time Joe or Sue leaves a comment, that action appears in the News Feeds of their connections—drawing more people to the discussion and to your profile (with its bread crumbs back to your business).

LinkedIn Company Profile

Companies also have profile pages and status updates, as seen in Figure 6.11. Individuals can follow companies and comment on their updates. To get double the traction, post your content to your company's profile (if you have one) and have your employees post the content to their profiles, too. In Figure 6.12, you can see Accounting Management Solutions' LinkedIn company profile.

LinkedIn Company Profile

Action	Appears in Company Profile	Appears on Followers' Feeds
Update Status	Yes	Yes
Comment on Status	Yes	Yes
Share a News Story	Yes	Yes
Add Apps to Profile (Blog, TripIt, etc.)	Yes	Yes
Add Jobs Function	Yes	Yes

Figure 6.11 Socially visible LinkedIn company profile activity

GOOGLE+ BUSINESS PAGE

A new social media platform, Google+ (Figure 6.13) is gaining traction, with over 40 million users as of October 2011.[4] The Google+ interface is very similar to that of Facebook but sorts each user's various connections into Circles. After adding Pages

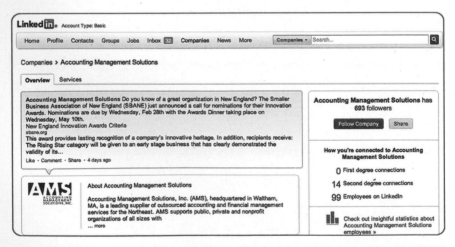

Figure 6.12 Accounting Management Solutions' LinkedIn company profile

[4]http://googleplus-update.blogspot.com/2011/10/google-plus-user-base-crosses-40.html.

Google+ Business Page

Action	Appears on Company Profile/ Stream	Appears on Followers' Profiles	Appears on Followers' Feeds
+1 the Page	Yes	Yes	No
+1 a Comment	Yes	No	No
Follower Shares a Story and Mentions Company (+1)	Yes	Yes	Yes
Add Company to Circles	Yes	Yes	No

Figure 6.13   Socially visible Google+ activity

and individuals to your Circles, you follow your connections' status updates, post updates to their profiles, and +1 their Pages or their comments. You can also add rich media to your posts, including photos and video, and create "hangouts" where you and your friends or customers can videos chat. (One small difference between Facebook and Google+: When you share links on Google+, you cannot edit them the way you can on Facebook.) You can expect that as traction builds on Google+, we will see even more ways to interact with different levels of social visibility.

As with the other platforms, Google+ status updates include a "share" button. The share is the most socially visible and complete way that someone can spread your content. When Joe shares your post, the people in his Circles see it, too. Figures 6.14 and 6.15 show an example of a Google+ Business Page for Shivagenic Photography—and one of the posts that's being shared.

ENCOURAGE SHARES TO HAPPEN NATURALLY

It should be very clear to you now that the share function is the key tactic for building socially visible content. So does that mean you

Figure 6.14 Shivagenic Photography's Google+ Business Page

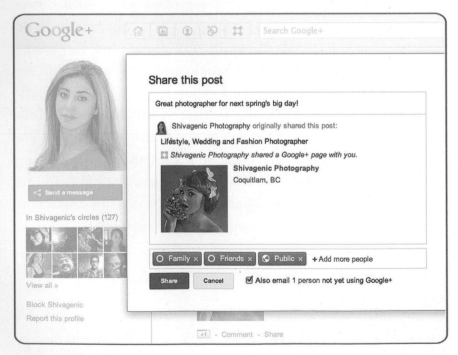

Figure 6.15 One of Shivagenic Photography's posts being shared

should ask for a share each time you post something? Absolutely not. If people love your content, they'll share it naturally.

Different people engage with content in different ways. Most people will Like, or +1, or leave a comment almost without thinking. Some people share a lot of content; others are more reticent. Asking them to share, however, significantly raises the engagement bar. When you ask people to share, you're asking them to explicitly promote your business to their networks. That's a form of endorsement, and while your fans might not call it that, they know it in their gut. Before they share, they'll pause to consider if this is a business or idea they are willing to be associated with.

Remember, we don't engage with (or endorse) businesses we don't believe in. When we share something about a business with our social circles, we're telling others that yes, we think this business is pretty cool—because we're willing to promote it via association. Asking people to promote your business again and again will make them feel uncomfortable and put upon, and this can cause them to opt out by removing you from their Circles, Unliking your Page, or unfollowing you on Twitter. So ask sparingly, but don't be afraid to ask!

When is the best time to ask for a share? When you have big news. A big product launch. A grand opening. Your annual campaign. A survey you're conducting for a high-level industry report. A great cause. You can also use natural sharing moments. Asking people to tell their networks that they're attending your event is one example of a natural share. Sharing the results of a poll or survey is another natural sharing moment. And you can ask people to share as a special favor if it's for a good cause. A pet store, for example, can ask people to share when someone's dog is lost and roaming the streets. Nonprofits can use this request a little more often than other types of businesses (but carefully).

Of course, developing content that people want to share helps *a lot*. High-level content that educates people almost always gets shared, as does free stuff, fun stuff, cool ideas, funny stuff, coupons, and events. The more visual and engaging content you post, the higher the shares. Videos often get shared. Infographics work. People will naturally share great content if it rises to the right level and is relevant to them and their friends. For inspiration, watch what pops up in your own Feeds. What types of content do people share and why? Test your theories and see if your customers share.

When your customers share, they're stoking your Engagement Marketing engine. They're helping you grow your business. Thanking them for their Likes, comments, and shares and making them feel like part of your community will go far in extending their initial WOW! experience. Engaging content will keep them coming back and will draw their friends in, as well. If one of your fans, followers, or connections goes above and beyond promoting your business without your prompting, give this person kudos with a personal thank you, an @mention, a link, or another form of recognition.

In the next chapter, you'll learn how two businesses and a nonprofit organization used Engagement Marketing to keep customers connected and grow revenues.

CHAPTER 7

ENGAGEMENT MARKETING IN ACTION

Real-World Examples

As a small business owner, you may already be doing pieces of Engagement Marketing and wondering how to tie everything together. Or you may be wondering how to get the cycle started—or even if what you're reading really works. In this chapter, we show you the money!

In the first example, you'll meet Bob Tullio of Gourmet Coffee Service, a small business in Southern California. Tullio had to think creatively in order to compete with national corporations that were gobbling up local coffee service businesses. Tullio's engagement strategy, which centered around an e-newsletter and a Facebook Page, didn't cost a lot of money or take much time—but it sure did net some fantastic results, including engaged clients, new business, and increased revenue.

Maas Nursery, a family-owned business in Houston, Texas, had to compete against the national big box chains. Cristina Maas Batz realized that she and her parents needed to step up their marketing efforts. The nursery used Engagement Marketing to create a community in which their customers would feel involved. Maas's engagement engine included an e-newsletter, on-site classes, a Facebook Page, and a Twitter account. Within two years, sales were up—a huge accomplishment in a down economy—and people who had never heard of the nursery were beating a path to its door.

Nonprofits often have to reach various audiences, such as bene-factors, potential members, and people who might attend the organization's events or fund-raisers. So their marketing has to do double duty while operating within a tight budget. Vicky Jaffe and her team at The Currier Museum of Art, located in Manchester, New Hampshire, used Engagement Marketing to fulfill its prime objective: to reach its audiences and get them engaged with the museum. The Currier's e-mail and social media programs keep people connected with the museum, keep them informed of news and events, and ultimately bring them back.

GOURMET COFFEE SERVICE ENGAGES CUSTOMERS, INCREASES MONTH-TO-MONTH REVENUES

Easy-to-implement tactics help Gourmet Coffee realize $100,000 in additional revenue in 11 months.

Founded in 1995 by Bob Tullio, VP of Business Development; his brother Pete Tullio, CFO; Jon Fishman, President; and Larry Deagon, VP of Operations, Gourmet Coffee Service deliv-ers office refreshment products and services to companies in the entertainment, legal, and finance industries. The company, which competes against national corporations, such as Aramark, Canteen Corporation, and First Choice, has grown from the ground up and now employs over 50 people, including drivers and four cus-tomer service representatives.

"Our biggest challenge is client retention and revenue generation," says Bob Tullio. "We have over 2,000 clients in the Los Angeles, Orange County, and Inland Empire areas. It's a huge territory—making it costly to maintain connectivity with decision makers. Our industry has seen lots of consolidation with the national coffee service companies gobbling up the smaller local ones. We knew remaining in touch with our customers had to go beyond the connection they had with our drivers."

DELIVER THE WOW!
SPOIL YOUR CUSTOMERS

Tullio and his team begin the Engagement Marketing Cycle by delivering a WOW! experience. Every four weeks, a driver arrives at a customer's workplace to restock the pantry using Gourmet Coffee's exclusive inventory control system and to clean and maintain the coffee brewer provided by the company. The driver even cleans the pantry!

"Our slogan is, 'We're going to spoil you,' and we do," says Tullio. "We really want to make our customers feel special. Exceptional service is one way to do that." Each Gourmet Coffee customer is assigned a dedicated client services representative. Each rep is responsible for being proactive by dealing with any special client needs, resolving pricing and product issues, and introducing new products and services. Reps visit each customer on a regular basis and manage quality assessment service surveys relating to driver route performance.

In fact, the company's mantra, "We're Going to Spoil You," extends far beyond the client services department. Each of Gourmet Coffee's team members understands that his or her job plays an important part in providing the highest level of service.

"Everyone here understands what, 'We're going to spoil you' means and works to provide it. That means that we look at the entire customer experience, from finding ways to keep costs down for customers to sending out easy-to-read invoices. Our goal is to make sure customers are so happy, they never want to leave." Now that's a WOW! experience!

ENTICE CUSTOMERS TO KEEP IN TOUCH

To further build connections with customers, Tullio turned to e-mail marketing. When the company was smaller, Gourmet Coffee was able to keep in touch with clients (and grow revenue) by sending free sample packets out with the drivers each month. Packets included new products, such as teas or coffees—and it was these samples that helped increase revenues each month as clients would often add the new products to their monthly list of Gourmet Coffee purchases. "As we grew, it became too costly and time consuming," says Tullio. Thanks to e-mail marketing, the free samples now arrive in customers' inboxes in the form of a Free Stuff e-newsletter that Tullio sends out once every six weeks.

The e-newsletter typically features two or three hot new products, such as wellness teas, biscotti, or eco-friendly cups and napkins. Customers choose what they want to sample and e-mail their requests back to the company. Reps handle the sample orders and ensure that customers get their "goody bags" when their driver next visits.

Gourmet Coffee also uses the newsletter to promote their other products and services, such as water filtration systems, single-cup brewing systems, vending machines, and more, which you can see

Figure 7.1   Gourmet Coffee's e-mail newsletter

in Figure 7.1. The company also has a "refer a friend" link in their e-newsletter. Customers who click on the link and refer a friend (typically via e-mail) to Gourmet Coffee receive a gift certificate. Tullio says the newsletter has been a great way to get Gourmet Coffee's product samples into customers' workplaces. "But we also use it to build connection," he adds. "Each newsletter includes a photo of one of our client service reps in order to give it that personal touch."

Tullio works with an employee to create "internal" content. "You have to walk a fine line between content that benefits your customers and content that's self-serving," he says. One issue, which tied into the company blog, featured an article on Gourmet Coffee's commitment to serving its community. The company provides all of the coffee—*gratis*—to Ronald McDonald House in Orange County as well as to two local youth organizations. "This lets our customers know we're involved in the community and also introduces these organizations to a wider audience," he says. "Again, it builds connection while promoting us as a company that provides more than just K-cups."

FACEBOOK PAGE GETS PEOPLE ENGAGED

Once he had his e-mail marketing program humming, Tullio turned his attention to Facebook. Tullio set up a Page (facebook .com/Gourmet-Coffee-Service) and drew over 300 fans within three months. Tullio and his partners committed to giving away $10,000 in prizes the first year by entering people who Liked the page in a weekly drawing. And we're talking some hefty prizes, too! An Apple TV, a giant smoker, and tool kits were just a few of the giveaways. For maximum traction, Tullio promoted the campaign via his newsletter as well (Figure 7.2).

"What really set off the Facebook Page growth and customer engagement," says Tullio, "was the driver contest." Gourmet Coffee encouraged customers to post comments about why they love their drivers. The top four drivers received a nice dinner at a local steakhouse. "We went from 150 to 350 fans in just three weeks with that contest," he says.

It takes Tullio a couple of hours a week to manage the Facebook Page. "I get a lot of industry newsletters with quirky stories," he

Figure 7.2 Gourmet Coffee promotes its Facebook contest in its e-mail newsletter

says, "so I just drop in the links and add a sentence or two of commentary. People love them."

One story from the *Chicago Tribune* reported that Starbucks would begin selling beer and wine at seven new stores opening in the Chicago area. Tullio's comment? "We were just in Chicago, so we get it. Someone will be in the first Starbucks bar fight ever. We'll be looking for that report."

Figure 7.3 Gourmet Coffee announces the weekly contest winner via video on Facebook

Tullio announced the weekly drawing winners through videos posted on the Facebook Page. In Figure 7.3, Pete, an employee, announces the weekly winner. Posting videos helped increase the fans' engagement activity, which made the Page even more relevant to its fans and helped ensure that Gourmet Coffee's content showed up in people's Facebook News Feeds.

ENGAGEMENT DRIVES NEW AND REPEAT BUSINESS

In just 11 months after implementing its Engagement Marketing engine, Gourmet Coffee realized more than $100,000 in additional

Figure 7.4 Gourmet Coffee's holiday coffee promotion

revenues. The refer-a-friend program netted dozens of referrals, with seven of them turning into accounts—which translated into an additional $5,000 per month.

"What happens," says Tullio, "is that we'll get over 100 sample requests each time we send out a newsletter. Between 30 and 40 percent of the samples are retained as ongoing products. So we can potentially generate $1,000 in new sales each month, and this is carried over month to month to month. For the December 2011 holiday season, we ran a special edition coffee promotion. We got a huge response: over 300 orders, a 100 percent increase over last year!" (Figure 7.4)

Figure 7.5   Gourmet Coffee's Engagement Marketing campaign components

When asked to share advice for other small business owners, Tullio replied, "Take it one step at a time. Set your objectives and then be patient. You have to let progress occur at its own pace. This approach to marketing—connecting with customers—does work. Stick with it and watch it grow."

As you learned from Bob Tullio, providing a WOW! experience makes it easy to keep in touch with your customers and clients. If your WOW! extends throughout your company, it will spill naturally into your Engagement Marketing. Sample goody bags, clean coffee pantries, and dedicated client service reps—why wouldn't Gourmet Coffee's clients want to keep in touch with the company and refer them to others? (See Figure 7.5.)

Similarly, Maas Nursery needed to find a way to connect with its customers, especially during a time when everyone was looking to save money and thus headed for the bargains offered at big box retailers. Instead of competing head-to-head on price, Cristina Maas Batz began building a community and invited people back to the nursery for hands-on gardening classes.

MAAS NURSERY CREATES A COMMUNITY AND GROWS ITS BUSINESS

Despite fierce competition, Maas increases revenue by 30 percent.

Competition with big box stores is Maas Nursery's main challenge. "We are more expensive than the big retailers," says Cristina Maas Batz, Marketing Director. "We get it. It's a tough economy and people want to save money wherever possible."

It was this challenge that spurred Batz to consider starting an e-newsletter in 2009. "Growing up, I didn't have much of an interest in the business," she says. "I went off to college for my degree and eventually got married. But then I became pregnant and quit my job. I had been thinking for awhile that I wanted to get in on the marketing side of things. Due to consolidation and competition with national chains, it's really tough for family-owned businesses to stay in business. It was very clear to me that we needed to step it up. We need to use technology to create a community where customers would feel like they were a part of our business."

MAAS WOWS CUSTOMERS WITH GARDENING EXPERTISE AND SELECTION

Maas Nursery is one of the few family-owned nurseries in the greater Houston area. Owned and managed by husband-and-wife team Jim and Carol Maas, and founded in 1951 by Jim's father, the garden center sits on 10 acres and carries everything from unique plants to unusual artifacts, antiques, and patio furniture. Many items are one-of-a-kind or are imported from Mexico.

The nursery is known for carrying plants and shrubbery that you won't find at the big box stores. In fact, their slogan is, "If you can't find it here, it probably doesn't exist!" Because Maas hires experts in their respective niches such as shrubbery annuals, or perennials, customers can bring photographs of their yards and get expert advice about what to plant and where. The company also provides landscaping and design consultation services. "We have a 365-day planting season," says Batz, "and people spend a lot of time and money on their yards. Often, they don't get the results they want. We help them reduce their costs and make their yards look much better."

MONTHLY E-NEWSLETTER PACKED WITH TIPS, COUPONS, AND OTHER GOODNESS

Batz's goal was to create an e-newsletter that educated people about gardening and plants as well as create a community that would draw others in. "I wanted the newsletter to be informative and a good resource for customers," she says.

The first issue, sent out in July 2009, was all this and more. Packed with helpful articles, the newsletter included top picks of the month, information on the different types of avocado trees the nursery had in stock, and a "buy one, get 20 percent off" coupon for customers who purchased a Cajun Hibiscus. Batz also included an article on the benefits of Maas Nursery's approach to landscaping, information on how to care for plants during the really hot summer months, and a recipe for zucchini brownies. ("If you grow vegetables, you know you always have way too many zucchinis," says Batz.) Maas Nursery employees helped write the articles; Batz gathered all the information and created the newsletter.

"That first issue was a little rough and a little ugly," laughs Batz, "but once I learned how to put things together, the look and feel improved. It also helped that I moved to Houston so that I could be

Figure 7.6 The July 2011 Maas Nursery e-newsletter

more hands-on with the marketing. Up until this point, I had been working remotely." Batz has been very consistent and produces the newsletter each month (Figure 7.6). Each issue is packed full of gardening and landscaping tips from Maas Nursery topic experts, an article written in Spanish for Maas's Spanish-speaking customers, and notices about upcoming classes. Each archived issue can be found on the Maas Nursery website (Figure 7.7).

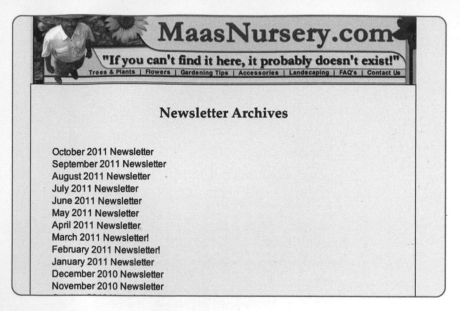

Figure 7.7   The Maas Nursery e-newsletter archive lets customers and prospects view the nursery's events and learn about plant/lawn care

EVENTS DRAW PEOPLE BACK TO THE NURSERY

To get people excited about gardening again and to reinforce a sense of community, Maas Nursery began offering classes on top-ics such as fall and winter gardening, container planting, and cacti and succulents. "We started doing events in the Fall of 2009," says Batz. "We'd promote the event through the newsletter and then people would e-mail us back to register. We've now automated that process using event marketing software." Each event is relevant to the season and features a 45-minute lecture and hands-on prac-tice. A big pot, soil, and the plantings are included in the $40 fee. "These events are a lot of work for us, and we give away $60 to $80 worth of stuff to each attendee. But we've had incredible turnout," says Batz. "We get lots of repeat customers, plus people come in who have never been to our nursery. Sales are always up by at least a third on class days." The nursery also hosts lectures and tours for gardening clubs.

It takes Batz approximately 15 hours a month to coordinate the newsletter and put it out. That time includes meetings, coming up with ideas, following up with people for their articles, and uploading the content. "We want as much employee involvement as possible," says Batz. "That way, the newsletter becomes personable, a local thing. People see an employee's photo and say, 'That's Kim, she talks about vegetables.'" An additional 10–15 hours per month are spent on class preparation. "That's start to finish," says Batz. "I do everything—from creating the event page and handling registrations to making sure we have enough materials."

ENGAGING CUSTOMERS THROUGH SOCIAL MEDIA

At the same time that she developed the e-newsletter, Batz began playing with Facebook. "Facebook is a great forum because more people interact on it," she says. For the Business Page, Batz focuses on seasonal planting tips, event notices, and weather alerts. "We're in a severe drought right now, the worst we've had in a hundred years. So we give people weather alerts as well as drought survival tips." A video of Jim Maas's appearance on a local TV station to talk about the drought netted numerous comments and a Facebook share. Batz often uploads photos of items from the nursery, too, and uses Facebook's Events feature to announce upcoming events (Figure 7.8).

"We've come to know the customers on Facebook, and then they show up at the nursery," says Batz. "It's been really good." A few months after she had Facebook up and running, Batz turned to Twitter (@maasnursery; Figure 7.9). Facebook, however, remains the nursery's destination of choice.

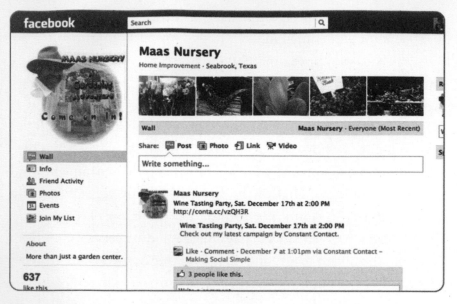

Figure 7.8   An event notice on Maas Nursery's Facebook Page

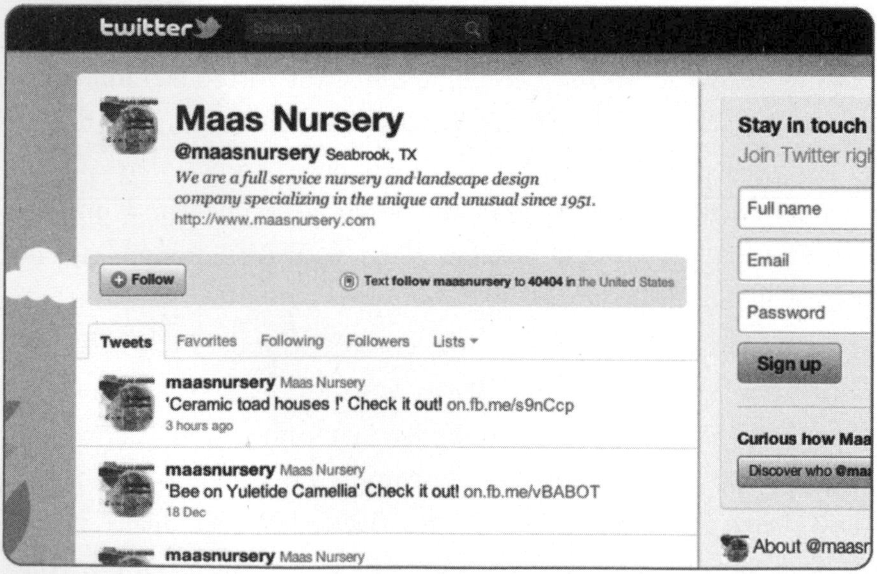

Figure 7.9   Maas Nursery's Twitter Feed

Figure 7.10   Maas Nursery's Engagement Marketing campaign components

SALES UP IN A DOWN ECONOMY; NEW PEOPLE VISIT

Engaging with customers through the e-newsletter, events, and Facebook (Figure 7.10) has paid real dividends, with sales up by 30 percent in 2011. "And this is in a down economy!" says Batz. "The e-newsletter, the events, and Facebook have been as effective as TV and radio, for much less cost and investment. People remember our name and tell others about us. Now we have new people coming to the nursery who didn't know we existed."

Her advice to other small business owners? "Use technology to expand your business. If I can do this, anyone can. I literally created newsletters and put the events together with my baby on my lap. Use your creativity and find ways to draw customers back to your business. Get your employees involved. Ask for their ideas. Have them write articles. The more your customers can relate to your business, the more they'll remember you—and come back when they need something."

If you're a nonprofit, community group, or association, you may be wondering how Engagement Marketing can benefit your organization. Actually, Engagement Marketing and nonprofits go together like bread and butter, a combination that the Currier Museum of Art has used to its advantage.

MUSEUM ENGAGES THE COMMUNITY, INCREASES ATTENDANCE TO PROGRAMS

Creativity and focus help Currier Museum of Art achieve a 27 percent increase in exhibition visitors

"People today have different ways of consuming information," says Vicky Jaffe, public relations and marketing manager for the not-for-profit Currier Museum of Art. "And who is online is constantly changing. Yesterday it was young adults; today older people are increasing in numbers online."

Reaching different audiences, engaging them, and ultimately bringing them back to the museum for exhibitions and events are the primary objectives for the Currier's marketing department. To accomplish these goals, Jaffe and her team rely on Engagement Marketing.

DELIVER THE WOW! EXHIBITIONS THAT ROCK, LITERALLY

The Currier often features New England artists; exhibitions range from photography and video to ceramics and, yes, rock and roll. In the *Backstage Pass: Rock and Roll Photography* special exhibition (October 7, 2011 to January 15, 2012) organized by the Portland Museum of Art, visitors were treated to 175 photographs, including studio shots and candid outtakes, drawn from the largest private

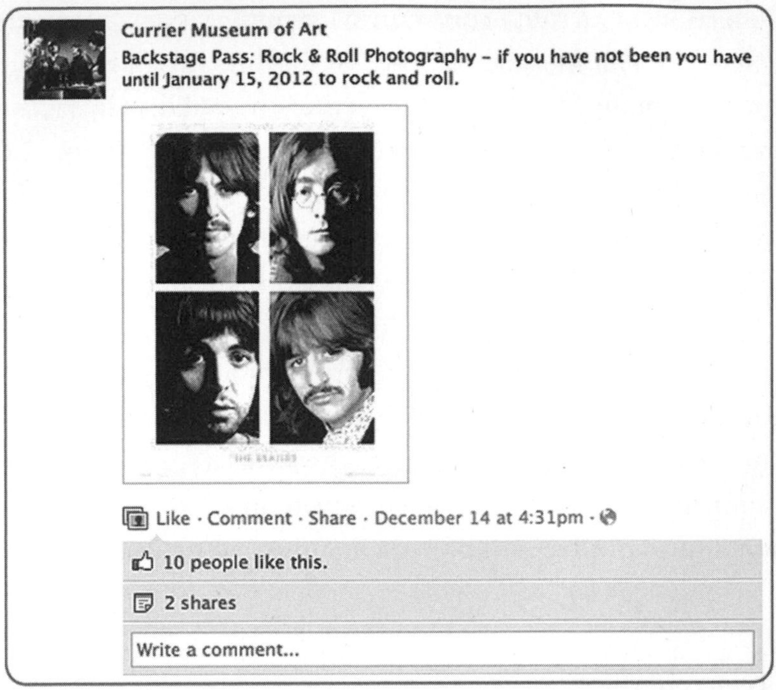

Currier Museum of Art
Backstage Pass: Rock & Roll Photography – if you have not been you have until January 15, 2012 to rock and roll.

Like · Comment · Share · December 14 at 4:31pm ·

10 people like this.

2 shares

Write a comment...

Figure 7.11 Currier Museum's Facebook post about the Backstage Pass exhibition

collection of rock musicians in the United States. Many of the photos had rarely been seen in public.

Response to and attendance at to the exhibition was fantastic. Fans shared their feedback on the Museum's Facebook Page, which you can see in Figure 7.11. This post, which shows off a photo of the Beatles, netted 10 Likes and two shares, further increasing exposure and accessibility to the Museum. Due to the exhibit, attendance was up from the same period a year before. Says Jaffe, "In November 2011, when the exhibition ran, 7,193 people visited the Museum, compared to November 2010 when 5,658 people visited—a 27 percent increase."

Since Currier's expansion in 2008, roughly 60,000 visitors a year have explored the Museum's world-class American and European art collections. Currier, located in Manchester, New Hampshire, also owns the Zimmerman House, the only Frank Lloyd Wright-designed home in New England open to the public. Currier's Art Center provides a year-round studio art curriculum for 2,000 students from 40 communities.

Currier is one of two large art museums with collections in New Hampshire, with the other museum located in Hanover, which is about a two-hour drive for people who live in the southern part of the state. "Because of our location—which is more urban—we have a large and diverse community," says Jaffe. "It's our mission to let the community know what's going on at the Museum and to invite them to participate in what we offer. To do this, we use a combination of e-mail and social media marketing."

MULTIPLE TOUCH POINTS KEEP PEOPLE CONNECTED AND INFORMED

The Currier has depended on e-mail marketing since 2004 and sends out its main e-newsletter, *eNews*, to over 7,000 subscribers on the first day of each month. The timing is especially important because the Museum holds its *First Thursdays Live* event on the first Thursday of each month. (Programming includes special exhibitions, gallery tours, a chance to mingle with other art patrons, and live music.) Each e-newsletter is packed full of news about exhibitions, tours, family events, art classes, and more. "We've had people opt out of receiving the print newsletter, so the electronic version, delivered on a monthly basis, keeps them connected," says Jaffe. The Museum also sends separate "e-blasts" to those who have chosen to receive news about the Museum's Art Center, which provides art classes, camps, and workshops for children, teens, and adults. In addition to the e-newsletters, the marketing team sends out targeted e-mails alerting people to exhibitions and other timely announcements.

One *eNews* that's a big hit every year is the Top 10 holiday gifts issue, which lists items available for under $20 at the Museum gift shop. According to Jaffe, people print the e-mail out and bring it with them to the shop. "That particular e-mail has definitely increased sales!" she says. As you can see in Figure 7.12, the e-mail lists some pretty cool and unique gifts—everything from artisan jewelry and knickknacks to toys and board games.

Figure 7.12   The Currier Museum's holiday gift guide *eNews*

SOCIAL MEDIA LETS PEOPLE "PLUG IN ON THEIR OWN"

The Museum set up its Facebook Page in 2009 and since then has seen it grow to over 2,800 fans. Topics run the gamut, from visitor feedback on exhibitions and reposts of Twitter content to announcements about scheduled events and "free to the public" viewing hours. "We get fairly good traction with Facebook," says Jaffe. Followers look forward to the "CMA Pick of the Week," a photo post in which a staff member poses with his or her artistic pick and shares information about the featured work. These posts not only pique people's interest and showcase the Museum's collection but also make art accessible and interesting to its fans—and anyone searching Facebook. In addition to its Pick of the Week, the Museum also posts notices of upcoming exhibitions, which helps to draw people back to the Museum, as seen in Figure 7.13.

Currier Museum of Art
Coming soon! A New Vision: Modernist Photography
Organized by the Currier Museum of Art
February 4, 2012 - May 13, 2012

This exhibition explores the critical and dynamic role photography played in the development of the Modern Art movement and the reciprocal influences among all media that shaped the modernist visual vocabulary.
...
See More

Currier.org
www.currier.org

The Currier Museum features European and American paintings, decorative arts, photographs, sculpture, and Frank Lloyd Wright's Zimmerman House – with exhibitions, tours, and performances year-round.

Like · Comment · Share · 11 hours ago ·

3 people like this.

Emily   Gotta see this too!
11 hours ago · Like · 1

Write a comment...

Figure 7.13   A Currier Museum event notice on Facebook

Figure 7.14   The Currier Museum's Twitter profile

The Currier marketing team uses Twitter to check into the larger world (Figure 7.14). The Museum follows local media outlets and organizations and responds to followers whenever the Currier is mentioned. The team repurposes content from both the print and e-newsletters as well as content from local publications for use on Facebook and Twitter. Jaffe and her team use hashtags when referring to exhibitions and events in order to solicit discussion. In addition to Facebook and Twitter, the Museum also manages a YouTube channel.

ENGAGEMENT ENHANCES ALL MARKETING EFFORTS; HELPS DRIVE ATTENDANCE

According to Jaffe, Graphic Designer Neva Cole manages the bulk of the Museum's Engagement Marketing efforts. "When Neva went on maternity leave, it took five of us to fill her shoes," she jokes. "Seriously though, we've learned that to manage everything effectively, you have to say, 'Okay, it's time to check in and take care of Facebook or Twitter.' You have to give it your focus.

"Every year, the makeup of people who go online changes," she adds. "More older people are online; younger people use Facebook more than e-mail. It's all very fluid. You can't ignore social media if you want to reach various types of audiences."

According to Jaffe, attendance at the Museum varies from year to year and month to month, often based on which exhibitions draw the most interest. The Public Programs team does surveys and asks visitors how they heard about the Museum. Jaffe sums up the results: "All of it—the newsletter, social media—it's all part

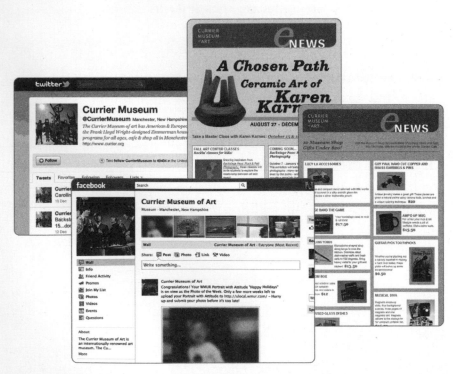

Figure 7.15   The Currier Museum's Engagement Marketing campaign components

of the mix. The e-newsletter complements Facebook and Twitter, and vice versa (Figure 7.15). It's definitely helped us reach various audiences, kept us in touch with them, and helped us bring them back to the Museum."

As you can see from these stories, Engagement Marketing is easy and fun. Start with one initial connection method, such as an e-newsletter or a blog, and once you have that piece in place and are gaining traction, add a social media platform, such as Facebook, LinkedIn, Google+, or Twitter. Engaging content is the centerpiece. Experiment with different content types. Then measure your results and repeat what works. If you have an Engagement Marketing success story that you want to share, visit our Facebook Page (www.facebook.com/constantcontact) and let us know! See more stories at engagementmarketing.com.

In the next chapter, you'll find five additional tips for increasing engagement. They're all easy to do and will definitely increase your Engagement Marketing fun quotient.

CHAPTER 8

ENGAGEMENT MARKETING TIPS AND TRICKS

I hadn't heard of The Beantown Sound, and neither had Melissa, an employee here at Constant Contact, until a photo appeared in her News Feed. Melissa's friend was tagged in the photo, which included a link to the event DJ's Facebook Page. Curious, she checked out its Page and learned that The Beantown Sound provides music and light shows for nonprofits, high schools, businesses, and consumers (think weddings). What we both loved, however, was The Beantown Sound's Facebook marketing. Owner Sam Lurie posts photo albums for each of his events and encourages people to tag themselves in the photos. When people tag themselves, The Beantown Sound's photos appear in their friends' News Feeds. Brilliant!

We've explained how you can grow your business by offering experiences that WOW! customers and by enticing them to keep in touch with you. We've shown you how small companies and nonprofits use content to engage people and drive social visibility. Now we'll share a few insider tips and tricks that further increase social visibility—and ultimately bring in new customers and prospects. All of them are easy, and, as in The Beantown Sound example, merely require some creativity, ingenuity, and fun.

TIP 1: MAKE YOUR CUSTOMERS THE STAR OF YOUR SHOW

When you highlight your customers or inspire them to post about their experiences, you bring your social presence to life. No one tells your story better than your customers. You also build stronger bonds with the customers in your photos—most people are excited to be featured. You guarantee some increased visibility, especially if you or your customers tag the people in the pictures.

When you ask your customers if you can take a quick picture for your Facebook Page (or interview them for an e-newsletter story, write a case study for your blog, or make them the featured client of the month), most people are flattered to be asked. Some will be too shy or private and will decline, but they will still be pleased that you asked. When you post their story, most people will also Like, comment, and share the story with their network. Along with this exposure comes implied endorsement from your customers. That's the power of social media!

Let's take another look at The Beantown Sound example. When the company posts its photo albums, the people in the photos tag themselves, an action that shows up in their friends' Feeds, as well. Figure 8.1 shows the second of two posts showcasing The Beantown Sound's photo album for a New Year's Eve event. Both posts netted a total of 29 shares. And what the screen shot doesn't show (which you would see if you clicked through to the album) is that 27 people tagged themselves and each photo has multiple comments and Likes. Yes!

If each of those 27 people has the typical 120 friends, then 3,240 people will potentially see the photo and the link to The Beantown Sound (plus the implied endorsement)! And a percentage of those people will visit the band's Page and Like it. When a

Figure 8.1   The Beantown Sound's photo album was shared by people who tagged themselves in the photos

new person likes the DJ's Page, that activity is recorded on his or her profile, further increasing Beantown Sound's social visibility. If The Beantown Sound is really lucky, one, two, or three people who see its Page (and event photos) will be planning an event and need a good DJ. Magic!

What's the best way to get people to share your content, check in at your business, or tag people in photos? One way is to make your customers the star of your show. When you include your customers or clients in your content, you'll tend to get more sharing (and more loyalty). If your business has a participation element, take pictures and videos as part of the fun. For the rest of us, it may take some creativity to make this strategy part of your Engagement Marketing plan. Can you possibly capture some of the WOW! experience moments you're creating? Perhaps you could take pictures at client meetings (that could be awkward) or ask your clients to do a short testimonial video at the end of an engagement. Or keep an inexpensive video camera handy (most of our smartphones qualify these days), and any time someone says something nice, ask them if they would mind repeating it for your Facebook or Google+ Page. Then let them know when and where you post it. They can't share if they don't know it's there!

TIP 2: CREATE PLATFORM-SPECIFIC CONTENT

Some people will connect with you using more than one channel. For example, some will sign up for your e-newsletter *and* connect with you on LinkedIn, or follow you on both Twitter and Facebook. Others might connect with you on all of your social networks and distribution channels. So it's a really good idea to create content unique for each platform, especially when you're promoting the same offer or event or sharing the same piece of information. Pushing the same exact post to multiple distribution channels makes it look like you're using old-fashioned mass marketing practices. It also gives the impression that you don't care about your content or your audiences—and dare I say it?—makes you look lazy. One-post-fits-all is definitely not what Engagement Marketing is all about.

Creating platform-specific content also allows you to take advantage of each platform's user expectations. Twitter is a broadcast mechanism and the ultimate short form. You want to carefully craft headlines that people will retweet. You want to focus on keywords people may be searching on, using any relevant hashtags and appropriate @mentions. Because it's more social and relaxed, Facebook gives you more space to work with. You can and should include pictures or images. Commenting is a natural part of the Facebook experience, so end your post with a conversation starter question. Even if you have a business audience, your fans expect you to show some personality and have some fun. LinkedIn is like going to a business networking event—your tone should be just as personable and friendly as on Facebook but more businesslike. In e-mail, focus on teaser content that gets people to click through and join the conversation on a social platform. Your content needs to be enough to pull them in, but keep it short and sweet and visually clean. Long e-mails get ignored! As of this writing, Google+ is still very new and in growth mode, so it's too soon to know how this new network will evolve, but for now, it feels like a cross between Facebook and LinkedIn—casual but businesslike.

To get people to engage with you—and stick with you—create content with each platform in mind. For example, if you're a yoga studio owner and you've written a blog post (your call-to-action destination) about the pose of the month, tweet a link back to the post. Your Facebook post will link back to your blog as well, but instead of a fast headline, you can give some insight into the benefits of this pose and include a picture with a call to action to read your blog post. If you're on LinkedIn and belong to a health and wellness group, you can write a post that ties into a previous discussion and add the link to your blog. Use your status update to alert your connections about your new post.

If you create content specific to each platform, the people who follow you on multiple platforms won't tune you out due to boredom or feeling spammed, and they'll look forward to reading—and sharing—your content in whichever way is easiest for them.

TIP 3: SEQUENCE YOUR POSTS

Another way to reach the broadest possible audience and avoid overload is to spread out your posts over time. Don't hit all your channels at once. Timing matters. If you hit your audience with content at a time when they're busy and not online, they'll likely miss it because your post will be pushed way down in their Feed by the next time they log in. This is why we recommend pushing your content out though multiple channels and at different times of the day. Remember that e-mail is the one channel where people will at least scan through every message. And, if you're sequencing the posts, you can use early engagement (Likes and comments) to make future posts more compelling.

While you can find a lot of data to suggest a "best time" for every channel, it makes sense to observe the response rates for your particular following and e-mail list. You should test different days and times to see which work best. Some things you want to consider: Schedule your short-lived social media posts to go out when your audience tends to be online. If you're a consultant on the East Coast and work with companies across the United States, those on the West Coast won't see your tweet from 7:00 AM Eastern time when they log on three or four hours later. If you write an e-newsletter or a blog post, time it to go live when you find you get the most opens and comments. If your call-to-action destination is Facebook, test whether posting at night or on the weekend gets you better response since some corporations block the platform. Conversely, if you have a business audience, posting to LinkedIn during the day may prove more beneficial. If you're selling to people or fund-raising across the United States or around the world, test time zones, too.

Key takeaway: Test various times to see when you get the best results for each platform. You can use automated tools such as HootSuite, TweetDeck, and Social Oomph to automatically send out posts that you've scheduled in advance. These tools provide analytics that tell you how many people clicked a link—and when. You can also use Facebook's Post Insights feature to determine the best times to post content.

And it's not just about timing: The order of your posts can matter as well. Start with your biggest audience or highest engagement channel (where you get the most comments or shares) so you'll have the best chance of getting traction. Once an engagement campaign gets some Likes and comments, spread it to other channels where that early engagement will help you get more pickup.

Tip 4: Fan the Flames of "Hot" Content

As your Engagement Marketing engine picks up steam, more people will begin engaging with you. A Google+, Facebook, or LinkedIn discussion will blossom, or a blog post will go viral and get double or triple the number of Likes, comments, retweets, or @mentions. When this happens, jump in and stimulate the conversation to keep it going. Respond and thank people for their comments. Ask follow-up questions. Stir the pot and see if you can keep the comments coming.

Use e-mail marketing and your other social media channels to draw people to the conversation. If you have a spirited discussion going, use Twitter, Facebook, and e-mail to invite people to join the fun. Let people know that the conversation is active. Tweet something like, "Wow! [name] blog post hit a nerve. Add your thoughts now. [URL link]." (See "Bitly" in Resources section for how to shorten URLs.) If your topic has people taking sides, add a poll to capture your fans' opinions, then do a follow-up post on the results. When the conversation begins to wane, restimulate it by going back through the thread and looking for related topics that were brought up but not fully developed to see if you can spark new conversations. Once you hit a rich area of interest, make sure you capitalize.

Stimulating and restimulating content increases engagement and drives still more social visibility. And content that engages has an additional benefit: It gets mentioned or picked up by bloggers and journalists as they add to or take issue with what's being said, which in turn sends new prospects to your door.

TIP 5: USE "LIKE-GATING" TO INCREASE PAGE LIKES

"Like-gating" is the practice of asking people to "Like" your Facebook Page. You encourage the "Like" by giving them something of value in exchange: a free report, some unique content, or a coupon, for example. Like-gating is similar to giving people an incentive to sign up for your newsletter list. Like-gating delivers your content to more users because it increases Page Likes, and when someone Likes your Page, that action appears on his or her Timeline or profile.

You can use Like-gating whether you're marketing to consumers, businesses, or donors. In Figure 8.2, Northrop Financial Group is offering information about free tax returns in exchange

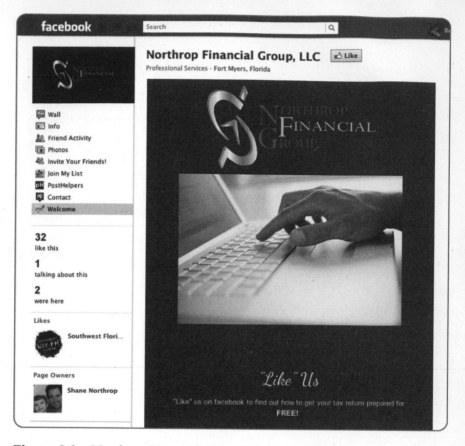

Figure 8.2   Northrop Financial Group offers the chance to get information about a free tax return in exchange for the Like.

for Liking its Page. This is a terrific example of a valuable offer that's highly targeted to the company's business audience.

In Figure 8.3, The Mountain Chalet also uses Like-gating effectively by offering people the latest news, events, and promotions in exchange for the Like.

Even nonprofits can use the tactic. In Figure 8.4, the Father-Daughter Ball asks for the Like.

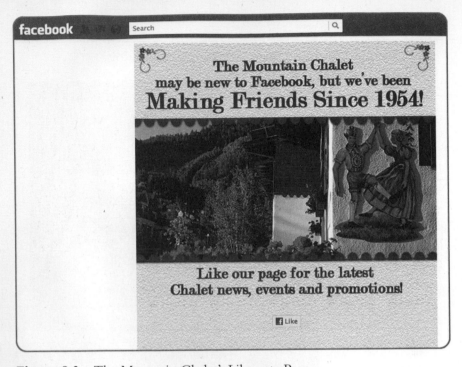

Figure 8.3   The Mountain Chalet's Like-gate Page

Photo Credit: Michael Brands; *Design Credit:* AZ Interactive Media

To ensure that you're getting targeted Likes—that the people who Like your Page might actually do business with you—your offer should be something of value that is related to your business, not something so general that everyone will want it (no contests to win iPads). You are trying to build a qualified audience who cares about your business or organization. For businesses working with other businesses, free reports or white papers, links to webinars, or special access to events work well. For consumers, discount coupons, notices of special sale days, or other incentives work well, too. And these offers don't have to be difficult or expensive to put together. You can bundle five of your most popular blog posts or e-newsletters into a special "tool kit" report, provide a link to a

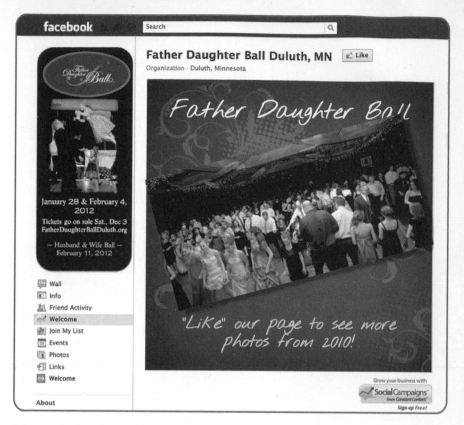

Figure 8.4 The Father-Daughter Ball Like-gate Page

special webinar or tele-class, or simply tell people they'll receive great content from you if they Like your Page—then be sure to follow through!

These tips will help you drive the engagement that results in a growing network of connected customers and prospects . . . and more business. In the next chapter, we explore some of the common obstacles to Engagement Marketing and how to overcome them.

CHAPTER 9

OVERCOMING COMMON OBSTACLES

"Okay," I can hear you thinking. "I understand why I should be doing Engagement Marketing. But let's get real. One, I don't have the time; and two, I already tried some of these things and they didn't work." When we talk to small business owners, these are two of the many objections we hear. In this chapter, we'll cover how to overcome the most common obstacles that most small business owners encounter when implementing Engagement Marketing:

Obstacle 1: "Too many different things to learn. Changing too quickly. I give up!"

Obstacle 2: "I don't have time."

Obstacle 3: "I don't like imposing on people."

Obstacle 4: "How do I find content ideas and inspiration? I'm not a marketer."

Obstacle 5: "I don't want to post personal information."

Obstacle 6: "My business is boring. Why would anyone follow us?"

Obstacle 7: "No one is reading my Facebook posts."

The good news is that you can easily rev up your Engagement Marketing engine using tools and tactics that don't take much time, special knowledge, or money.

OBSTACLE 1: "TOO MANY DIFFERENT THINGS TO LEARN. CHANGING TOO QUICKLY. I GIVE UP!"

We understand. You're running your business, you have customers to serve, and you're putting out fires. Technology is rapidly changing, and a new social media platform or tool seems to appear almost every day. On top of that, you're a little overwhelmed by all the terms being bandied about: Likes, followers, Klout scores, retweets, +1s, status updates, DMs. It's at this point that you give up—without even starting. When it all gets too confusing, you give up before you even start.

The key is to start small. Master *one* new thing. Begin to build some engagement. Think "quality" versus "quantity." Get your e-mail newsletter going, and pick one social network as your engagement destination rather than trying to develop two, three, or four all at once (especially if you're just starting out).

Quality Versus Quantity

While the press focuses on those social media outliers with thousands (or millions) of fans and followers, the vast majority of small businesses are just getting started and have very modest numbers. A recent review of Constant Contact's customers showed that 65 percent had fewer than 250 Facebook fans. But their numbers are growing daily. The only way to grow a larger following is to start small and grow from there. You may never get thousands of Facebook Page Likes or newsletter subscribers, and that's okay.

Instead of worrying about numbers, focus on enticing and engaging the people you do know. Remember, your current customers or clients have social networks full of great prospects for your business. What you want to shoot for is quality. Get the people you already do business with to connect with you, and their engagement will spread the word about your business to their friends, families, and colleagues. Work to increase engagement with those who have connected with you and figure out what types of content will get them to Like, comment, and share.

Start Testing Content Types and Grow From There

As we said in Chapter 5, any engagement is fantastic. It takes some time and testing to find the right types of content to inspire action. Check out the different types of engagement content in Chapter 4, and pick one to start. Try something. If you have people retweeting or linking to your content, Liking or commenting on your Facebook or Google+ Page, or joining your LinkedIn Group, then you're on the right track. Use your "small" successes as a foundation for building momentum. As we've said throughout this book, engagement builds over time. No matter how many people follow you on any platform, only a small percentage will engage with you at any given time. If you share something on Facebook and five people Like it and two people leave a comment, that is wonderful! You have engagement, which in turns drives social visibility and draws even more people to your business.

Focus on One Initial Engagement Destination

As we discussed in Chapter 2, it's much easier to focus on building out one connection point or destination (e.g., your e-mail newsletter, Facebook or Google+ Page, LinkedIn Group, or Twitter presence) instead of trying to build out two, three, or four all at once. This strategy not only lowers your learning curve and helps you get comfortable but also concentrates your audience and helps you drive some initial critical mass. It is far better to have 100 followers all on Facebook than 25 followers in four different places. Start where you find the biggest concentration of your customers or where they are most comfortable connecting (hint: E-mail is often the most comfortable starting point).

If, after examining what works for your customers, you've determined that an e-newsletter and Facebook are the best tactics for you, focus on making both the best they can be. If LinkedIn is your starting point, dive in there. Take the time to learn how to use the tools, maybe attend a few seminars or webinars. Observe how others are using them. Engagement will build, and as you become more successful (and confident), you can add other tactics or platforms such as a blog, Twitter, or Google+.

OBSTACLE 2: "I DON'T HAVE TIME."

As we will outline below, you can rev up your Engagement Marketing engine in as little as 15 to 20 minutes a day. The trick is to consistently spend some time every day (or at least a few days a week) creating or posting content and responding to followers. Again, focus on your preferred destination to keep things simple and prevent getting overwhelmed. To overcome the "I don't have time" challenge, reread Chapter 8 and incorporate one or more of the tips and tricks outlined. You can also consider setting up a schedule, getting help from employees, or outsourcing.

Not all of your content needs to be original. In addition to your own updates, you can share interesting content from others. The industry now calls this "curating content." The key here is to set up some monitoring tools to follow relevant keywords, blogs, companies, and individuals. There are a few tools listed in Chapter 10, and you can find more resources at engagementmarketing.com.

You'll quickly find great people writing about your focus area who are completely noncompetitive. Share their articles, Facebook posts, blogs, or Google+ posts (with complete attribution) and add some commentary or discussion starters. Your clients view of you as an expert, sharing the best of your industry is part of your value-add. Sharing others' content has the added benefit of connecting you with the authors, if they happen to see that you have shared or retweeted their content. Who knows, maybe they will follow you back and share some of your content with their audience in the future.

Set Up a Schedule

If you're like many of the business owners we work with, you do your marketing whenever you can squeeze in half an hour here or there. To really get your Engagement Marketing engine humming, set up a scheduled time to work on social media to help you get going and remind you to give it some focus. In a perfect world, you would set aside a few minutes at the beginning of each week to plan out your Engagement Marketing activities, starting with any business events you want to highlight (i.e., you're having a sale, your newsletter is going out, your blog post is going live, you have a special report that's ready to go, it's the big game on Sunday and you have specials, you attended an expo and have news on exciting trends). Your plan doesn't have to be complicated or take hours to develop—think "back of the napkin." Your goal is to be consistent without having to spend a whole lot of time. Concentrate on planning one or two original content spots to anchor your week and fill in the rest with curated content.

Your schedule and plan should also include a little time every day to check in online and see if you have any new comments or posts, welcome new fans and followers, and generally be present.

This is especially true when you've just posted a question or conversation starter; discussion needs to be nurtured. With smartphones, it's easy to check in any time you have a spare moment in your day.

And while you may have a plan for your engagement, you should be ready to post news "as it happens." For example, let's say you're the owner of a trendy clothing boutique. As you scan through celebrity sites, you run across a picture of a movie star wearing a belt that your boutique just happens to carry. By all means, quickly post a link to the image and let your customers know that you have this fabulous belt in stock! If something big happens in your industry, a new report full of meaty data comes out, or something fun or interesting is happening right now at your place of business, post about it ASAP. Don't tell yourself you'll "do it later." Tasks and fires and customer requests will pile up, and you'll forget; and by the time you remember, the news won't be as fresh. Once you are familiar with a particular platform or tool, posting your news should only take a minute!

As we discussed in Chapter 8, consider timing, the platform, and your audience. Just because you're writing your content at 10:00 PM doesn't mean this is a good time to post it. If you're targeting businesspeople, they may check Twitter, LinkedIn, or Google+ throughout the day but not Facebook (as some corporations block it). Stay-at-home moms and college students may be on Facebook throughout the day, while teens won't log on until after school and will stay on well into the late evening. And don't forget the weekends—you may get better traction posting on a Sunday or even a holiday than on a weekday. So how can you achieve maximum visibility and still work on social media during your own downtime? Free or low-cost tools, such as Hootsuite, TweetDeck, and Social Oomph, let you schedule posts to major platforms (such as Facebook, Twitter, LinkedIn, and Foursquare) in advance.

Enlist Your Employees

To make your Engagement Marketing campaigns more fun, ask your employees for their ideas, inspiration, and help creating content and responding to followers. You personally may not like writing Facebook posts or an e-newsletter, but you may have one or two employees who love it . . . by all means, let them help! You can include your employees in your weekly Engagement Marketing strategy sessions (bring coffee and pastries and watch the ideas flow) or let them respond to Twitter @mentions and retweets, post status updates, and monitor review sites. And, if your employees are a little more socially savvy than you are, they can show you how to set up a profile, respond to a tweet, or leave a comment on a blog post. (If you're a one-person business and you're nervous about setting up your first social network profile, you can hire a consultant to show you how it all works, too. Or check out Constant Contact's Social Quickstarter at www .socialquickstarter.com.)

Outsource It

Outsourcing your Engagement Marketing activities comes with pros and cons. In general, be cautious with outsourcing. The benefit, of course, is that you don't have to do it yourself or learn anything new, which frees you up to focus on your business. This works especially well if you're a "mobile business," meaning you're in the field or with clients all day.

The biggest (and most obvious) disadvantage to outsourcing is that the consultant or agency overseeing your account isn't you. That means they won't know which content really matters. Or what's happening in your business. And they won't sound like you—your business's personality won't come through in their posts. They don't know your customers, so they can't respond as you would when your best client posts something. You won't get to know your customers and clients through the one-to-one interactions that take place on social media.

Another disadvantage is that you may lose control over your profiles. If you do outsource your Engagement Marketing, make sure the consultant or agency sets up your profiles using your name and password. This is especially true for Facebook. If a consultant sets up your Page using her Facebook profile, you may not be able to access the Page from your own account. You'll lose your Page—along with all the social visibility you've built—should the consultant decide to go out of business, get a "real" job, or just flake out, never to be heard from again (yes, this happens).

OBSTACLE 3: "I DON'T LIKE IMPOSING ON PEOPLE."

As we discussed in Chapter 3, some small business owners don't like asking customers and clients to keep in touch with them. "I don't want to bug people" is the common refrain we hear. We get it. But if you don't ask, you will never grow your connections and build your business with Engagement Marketing. Asking people to connect with you will get easier with practice as you build your enticement muscles, so to speak. It's much easier if you have confidence in the value that you are delivering (see Obstacle 6). As with any new activity, you have to do it consistently in order to feel comfortable. One way to overcome the "I'm imposing" feeling is to make it a daily practice to ask people to connect with you. Some ways to build a daily routine include setting goals, making enticement everyone's job, and setting up a great enticement offer.

Set Goals, Run Contests

Set weekly or monthly goals for adding newsletter or blog subscribers, Page Likes, +1s, or retweets/@mentions. If you want to double your e-newsletter subscriber list in six months, break it down by working backward: If you already have 300 subscribers, you'll need 300 new subscribers, which translates to 50 per month, 12 per week, or 2 per day. Easy! If you have employees, run contests to see who can get the most Page Likes, e-mail addresses, or new followers in a week.

Make It Easy and Fun to Connect

As we've already discussed, make it easy and fun for people to keep in touch with you. Include your newsletter subscription form on your website, blog, and Facebook Page. Include a link on your LinkedIn profile and Corporate Page as well. Keep your subscription form short and sweet. You can add your blog to your Facebook Page, Google+ profile or Business Page, and LinkedIn profile. If you allow comments on your blog, make it easy to leave a comment. Don't use a program that forces people to log in or register. Include your Facebook, LinkedIn, or Twitter URL on business cards, e-mail signatures, invoices, packaging, signage, and on your website or blog.

Have a Great Enticement Offer

Once you've made it easy to keep in touch with you, tell people what they'll get for joining. Try to think of something that offers immediate value, such as a free report, a coupon, an e-course, or a recorded webinar. Or, if it works for your business, give people a discount if they check in via Facebook or Foursquare. Make your content fun and unique—something they'll get only if they decide to connect with you. Make people feel good and excited about keeping the connection and receiving content from you. Stay focused on offers that relate directly to your business, and use them as a qualifier. If the only reason people connect is to win an iPad, that is not an engaged audience. See Chapter 3 for additional details about enticing people to keep in touch.

OBSTACLE 4: "HOW DO I FIND CONTENT IDEAS AND INSPIRATION? I'M NOT A MARKETER."

Inspiration is all around you if you remember that imitation is the sincerest form of flattery. So many companies are doing great things with social media and marketing in general that you don't have to come up with new ideas yourself. Just watch what others are doing, and adapt these ideas to work in your business. Sign up for blogs and e-mail lists, "Like" Pages of companies outside of your industry, and follow companies and brands on Twitter. Look for the activities that get a lot of engagement (Likes, comments, retweets, etc.). Why do you think that content worked? How could you do something like that for your business?

One important tip: when you see something good, make a note of it! You won't remember it a week from now. You can start an old-fashioned paper folder or an online folder. If you see something you like, take a screen shot and/or print it out. I personally keep an e-mail folder of cool marketing ideas of all types that I find interesting or think we could try someday. I'll take screen shots and e-mail them to myself, send myself a link to a site, or even take pictures of direct mail pieces. Watch how other companies use questions to engage people on Facebook, start LinkedIn polls to generate interest, or create reports, webinars, and events. Have fun with this; encourage other people to send you things they see and like. Then, when you're stumped for content, pull out the file and try one of those great ideas in your Engagement Marketing.

OBSTACLE 5: "I DON'T WANT TO POST PERSONAL INFORMATION."

We still hear this objection regarding social media on a regular basis. Small businesspeople see others sharing where they're going for dinner or stuff about their personal lives and think, "I don't want to share that information." I don't blame you. It creeps me out, too. Yes, some people do overshare, but *you* don't have to. You do need to show some personality, but your content can stay strictly business, especially if you're creating content that goes out under your business name (or your own name, if you're a one-person business).

While privacy is important, including some personal details can make your content more engaging and create a sense of connection with your audience. Determine what you will and will not talk about. Some people are much more open than others with regard to their lives. But keep it relevant to the reason they connected with you in the first place. If someone is following you for business advice, they probably don't care about your nephew's high school graduation. Unless your business is about you, draw a clear line for your content. And unless politics and religion are your topic areas, it's best not to veer into these dangerous waters. It's really up to you and what you feel comfortable doing. No hard-and-fast rule exists about how much of yourself you should expose online. Bottom line: If it makes you feel uncomfortable, don't do it.

OBSTACLE 6: "MY BUSINESS IS BORING. WHY WOULD ANYONE FOLLOW US?"

While your topic area may be dry, your Engagement Marketing does not have to be. You can make *any* area interesting with some good content, delivered with personality. If your content is not naturally engaging, you'll have to work harder to find ways to draw in and engage an audience. We talked about content ideas in Chapter 4. Go back through those ideas with an eye toward your specific content. Is there a way to make it fun? To break it down into more digestible pieces and maybe add a quiz or survey? Start a boring industry trivia contest? Ask people to try to "stump the expert?" You get the idea: take something serious and make it fun. But stay true to your content and audience.

You are not the only person with this challenge, so watch what other companies in your industry and other similarly "boring" businesses are doing.

It also helps to have an online personality for your business. Sometimes dry material is greatly improved with a little personality. When you begin your Engagement Marketing, take a few minutes to jot down your business's personality traits and the tone you'll use: happy, witty, personable, irreverent, knowledgeable, friendly, and so on. Then, be your business. Show your company's personality—or authenticity—and have some fun doing so. Remember, people do business with people. The more they get to know you (and your company and its employees), the more they'll come to trust you, and the easier it will be for them to share your content and refer you to others.

OBSTACLE 7: "NO ONE IS READING MY FACEBOOK POSTS."

It's difficult to tell who is reading or even seeing your Facebook posts. Sometimes you post things and nothing happens. Then you ask one of your favorite customers (or your spouse or business partner) what they thought, and you discover that they didn't even see it. Two big factors are at play here: Crowded News Feeds and the ever-changing formula Facebook uses to decide what to put in each individual's News Feed.

People are using Facebook (and other social networks) to connect to more people and businesses than ever before. In February 2010, Facebook had over 400 million users; by December 2011, that number grew to 800 million.[1] As a result, people have so many posts and comments flowing into their Feeds that they may not see yours, especially if they don't check Facebook around the time you posted. By the next time they connect, many other posts will have risen above yours, and they may never scroll down to see what happened hours ago. That's why you want to be thoughtful about timing; post to multiple channels and at different times as we discussed in Chapter 8. You want to increase the odds that your audience will catch your content.

The second factor at work here is that Facebook is working hard to make sure they deliver the most relevant content to each individual. If Facebook deems your content unworthy, it may not even be showing up at all! The factors, influences, and rules that Facebook use to decide what content to deliver make up the EdgeRank algorithm.

EdgeRank is Facebook's closely guarded News Feed filtering algorithm. Every single thing that happens on Facebook is

---

[1]www.facebook.com/press/info.php?timeline; Facebook, December 2011, http://newsroom.fb.com/content/default.aspx?NewsAreaId=22.

considered an "Edge": Liking a comment or Page, commenting, checking in, and posting photos and videos all add an edge to your content. Your "EdgeRank" goes up as you gain more interaction. However, EdgeRank is person-specific. Status updates from "close friends" or "friends" appear at the top of a user's News Feed. So if your content appears at the top of my News Feed, that means I'm probably Liking or commenting on your status updates and photos on a regular basis. This improves your EdgeRank, and I see more of your updates in my News Feed, because Facebook has determined that you are relevant to me.

However, if your friends or acquaintances continually ignore your posts, they'll see fewer of them (if any) because Facebook has determined that you're not relevant to these people. In other words, you show up less and less in your friends' News Feeds—and you won't even know it. (If your teenager says she never sees your posts, now you know why!)

It works the same way for the Page for your business or organization: You could have 250 Page fans but only a percentage of them see your posts. This is because Facebook measures how "engaging your posts have been to Facebook users over a rolling seven-day window." They also score your content with an algorithm that takes into account your "number of posts, total fan interactions received, number of fans, as well as other factors."[2] It's not worth your time trying to understand the algorithm (it is confidential and it changes all the time). The bottom line is that Facebook measures engagement. This is why creating engaging content is so crucial and why using Facebook for the call-to-action is so valuable. Every action your followers and friends take adds to your EdgeRank.

---

[2]www.facebook.com/help/search/?q=post+insights.

It's also why it makes sense to have other ways to connect with your audience and pull them back into Facebook. If Facebook is your only channel and you're no longer showing up in someone's Feed, you've become invisible to that individual. You have, essentially, lost that connection. If you also have a way to send them that content via e-mail, then you have another chance to connect.

Generating engagement on Facebook isn't easy, and it can take a while to build a community of engaged fans, but the effort is worth it. There's no denying that Facebook has traction across all demographics in the United States and around the world.

Hopefully this chapter has addressed some of the common obstacles to Engagement Marketing. In the next chapter, we will point you to some resources that can help as well.

CHAPTER 10

RESOURCES

In this chapter you'll find a few tools, tips, and tricks, and a glossary that may be of assistance as you fire up your Engagement Marketing engine. You'll also find lots of up-to-date information at a resource center developed specifically for small business owners: engagementmarketing.com. This site is not only a source of information but also a destination for discussion, sharing best practices and, you guessed it, engagement. Be sure to check it out!

SOCIAL MEDIA QUICK-START GUIDE

We know that when you're new to social media, learning how the various platforms work can be a little daunting. In this section you'll find a brief, basic overview of the "Big Four" platforms (Facebook, Google+, LinkedIn, and Twitter), explanations for the various terms associated with each platform, and tips for using some of the platforms' features.

FACEBOOK

The largest of the social networks, Facebook (http://facebook .com) has become a favorite destination for people, businesses, and organizations to connect and share information because of its easy-to-use interface and interactive features. Facebook is multimedia-friendly as you can post text, pictures, audios, and videos. The platform also offers tons of applications and widgets that can make your Facebook Page engaging and fun.

Commenting

Just about everything posted to Facebook has a comment field for you, friends, and fans to post a response and facilitate a conversation. (Also see "Comments" in the Glossary.)

Fan

"Fan" was previously used to refer to a user who chose to connect with a Page. Facebook no longer uses this term; currently, when someone chooses to connect with a Page, he or she "Likes" it, rather than "becoming a fan." (See "Like.") While most people will know what you mean when you ask them to "become a fan" on Facebook, the preferred terminology is for you to ask someone to "follow," "friend," or "Like" you on Facebook.

Friend

To connect with someone on Facebook through a personal profile, you "friend" them. The friend connection is two-way, meaning both parties have to agree before the connection is made. (See also "Unfriending.")

Help Center

The best place to get help with Facebook is the Facebook Help Center (www.facebook.com/help). You'll find a plethora of information about setting up an account, managing your profile and

Business Page, privacy settings, and links to mobile apps. You can access the Help Center by clicking the little "down arrow" in the right corner next to "Home." The Help Center is listed at the bottom of the drop-down menu.

Highlighted Stories

These are stories marked with a blue corner in your News Feed. Facebook determines which stories get highlighted based on a number of factors, including "your relationship to the person who posted the story, how many comments and Likes it got, what type of story it is, etc."[1] A story that might not normally be highlighted may be highlighted if it has multiple comments and Likes.

Like

The "Like" button is now ubiquitous on (and off) Facebook. The Like button provides a simple way for Facebook users to share their approval or endorsement with their network of friends. Users can Like a Page as a way of giving a recommendation, or they can simply Like an individual post, picture, or video to provide a virtual thumbs-up.

You may have noticed Like buttons on websites outside of Facebook. These are a great way to get customers who visit your website or blog to recommend your business or to get an individual to post to their Facebook network. You can also add a Like button to your e-mail newsletter to help amplify your voice and extend your message beyond the in-box.

You can learn how to add a "Like" button to your website here: www.facebook.com/badges.

---

[1]https://www.facebook.com/help/search/?q=highlighted+stories

Message

Messages are private notes sent between users. They're only viewable to the sender and recipients. It's pretty much like sending an e-mail, but the address book is limited to your Facebook friends. Note: Facebook does not allow you to send a private message to any user who Likes your Page. You must be connected as friends in order to exchange private messages with another user.

News Feed

The content that your friends and the businesses or organizations you Like post on Facebook goes into your News Feed. The News Feed is the basic landing page that individuals see when they log into Facebook.

Page

A Page (previously referred to as a fan or Business Page) is the recommended platform for your business or organization to connect with new people and engage with your existing customers in an open dialogue. The benefit of a Page is that customers can follow it by hitting the "Like" button. Unlike the friend connection, Likes don't have to be reciprocated.

When you post a comment to your Page, it will show up in your fans' News Feeds. You can create an incredible network effect by posting interesting and valuable content and promotions to your Page, which is then shared by your fans.

Page Insights

Want to know how many people actually viewed your Page, checked in, or shared posts? Want to know which posts generated lots of engagement and which didn't? You can see all of this activity via Facebook's nifty Insights feature. You can access this feature very easily: Go to your Page and in the left margin, look for "Insights."

On Insights, you can view tabs for Likes, reach, Page analysis, and check-ins. If you're not sure what something means, hover over the little question marks and a box will pop up with explanations for each data point.

Page News Feed

Want to follow other businesses but don't want to clog up your News Feed on your own personal profile? You can, by accessing your Business Page's News Feed. Go to your Page and click "Use Facebook as [your Page name]." Now when you Like other Pages, their posts will appear in your Page's News Feed. To access your Page's News Feed, click "Home" while you're still logged in as your Page name.

Personal Profile

Any individual who is on Facebook has a personal profile; it's the focal point for the entire network. Your profile page contains all your pertinent information, and is how others find and connect with you personally on Facebook.

On your profile, you can share status updates, photos, videos, links, and other content. Plus, friends can comment on your posts. Businesses, organizations, and celebrities are recommended to create a Page rather than a personal profile.

Share

Sharing is synonymous with posting or publishing. You can publish text, links, photos, videos, and events on Facebook using the share box at the top of your profile. After entering your text, you have the option to upload a photo or video or insert a link. When you share a link, Facebook will automatically include the title, description, and an image (if available) from the Page you're linking to. If multiple images exist on the Page, you have the option to select which image you want to use as the thumbnail. You can also change the specific text that is displayed by clicking on it.

In addition, when you share content on your Page, your fans and friends can then Like, comment on, or share the content with their friends. The share feature is what makes publishing content to Facebook so powerful. By sharing great content, you can encourage your friends and fans to syndicate your message, creating a powerful network effect. (Also see "Sharing" in the Glossary.)

Tag

You can tag friends in pictures, places, videos, and text posts. Tagging places a link from the item to the tagged person's profile. Tagging a person in one of your own photos may allow that person's friends to see your photo, depending on the tagged person's privacy settings.

Ticker

The Ticker is Facebook's "real-time" News Feed. It appears on the right side of the screen, above the chat bar. Your Likes, comments, and shares appear in your friends' Tickers. You only see the Ticker on your home page if you've Liked a number of Pages, use a lot of apps, or are a heavy Facebook user. In other words, not everyone has one, so don't worry if you don't see the Ticker.

Timeline

Timeline is Facebook's latest feature that replaces the traditional Wall for both profiles and Pages. Timeline is a graphic representation of people's Likes, comments, interests, photos, and activities on Facebook. For Business Pages, Timeline includes the same graphic updates and also some new functionality for Pages (i.e., fans can privately message Page admins, Welcome Pages have been removed). See also "Wall."

Unfriending

You can "unfriend" someone to disconnect with them on Facebook. When you unfriend someone, the person is not notified that you have done so.

Wall

As of this printing, personal profile Walls and Business Pages have been replaced by Timeline. When people write updates on your Business Page Timeline, these updates are publicly visible. For personal Timelines, what is public depends on your individual privacy settings. See also "Timeline."

GOOGLE+ (G+)

Google+ (http://plus.google.com) is Google's relatively new social media platform. As with Facebook, you can set up personal and business profiles, post content that includes links, photos, and videos, and "+" (tag) people and businesses that are on the Google+ network. Commenting and sharing work the same way that they do on Facebook, so if you haven't already, read the preceding section for additional insights. (Also see "Comments" and "Sharing" in the Glossary.)

Circles

Circles are Google's way of categorizing the people you're following. You can create as many Circles as you like and name them whatever you want. You can add individuals to multiple Circles, a useful feature if you have a friend who is also a business colleague.

When you write a new post (either for your Page or your profile), you can select which Circles should see the post. For example, if you're posting a picture of your kids, you can select just your "friends" and "family" Circles so that only they will see your post.

To send a private message, delete the green "Public" button, then type in the person's name from your Circles. Only the intended recipient will be able to see your message. To tag someone in your Circles, add a "+" before that person's name.

Hangouts

This app allows you to video chat with one or more people.

Page

Pages are the preferred format for businesses to establish a presence on Google+. Similar to Google+ profiles, you can add photos and videos, to your Page as well as text content. People can follow your Page by adding it to their Circles. As the business owner, you can set up Circles on your Page and add people to them.

Plus One (+1)

The "plus one" button is very similar to Facebook's "Like" button. You can +1 a Business Page, a post, or a comment. The +1 button can be added to web pages and blog posts to encourage people to interact with your content. You can also find +1 buttons in Google's search results next to each listing on the search engine results Page. When you "+1" a website, blog post, or Page, this action appears on your Google+ profile.

Profile

Similar to Facebook's Wall or Timeline, the Google+ profile includes your posts, your information, photos, videos, and any Google+ pages or website pages you've added using the +1 feature.

Stream

The "Stream" is your Feed of posts from people in your Circles.

LINKEDIN

Often described as the most professional of the big three social media networks,[2] LinkedIn (http://linkedin.com) lets you connect with friends, colleagues, and other people with whom you've worked or done business. Your LinkedIn profile is akin to an online resume; the network even allows others to write recommendations for you. As on Facebook, connections made on LinkedIn must be verified by both parties. Companies can have their own profile pages on the site, and Group features let you build discussion areas around a central topic.

Applications

LinkedIn allows you to add various functions to your profile through its applications feature. For example, you can add your

---

[2]Facebook, Twitter, LinkedIn.

WordPress or TypePad blog, which automatically updates when you post something; add books to your Reading List (very nice for those who read a lot); use TripIt to tell your network when and where you're traveling (a great way to set up meetings with people, as others can see your location and contact you if you're coming to their area); and add presentations with SlideShare (http://www.slideshare.net).

These applications are very easy to use and don't require any technical knowledge.

Companies

Similar to the Facebook Page or Google+ profile, company Pages are designed for businesses who want to establish a presence on LinkedIn. Company Pages can be used to list all of your employees who have personal accounts on LinkedIn.

Connections

LinkedIn has three degrees of connection. First-degree connections are people who you have mutually agreed to connect with on the network. Second- and third-degree connections are people who are connected to your first-degree connections, but not directly with you. One of the benefits of LinkedIn is that first-degree connections can introduce you to second- and third-degree connections.

Groups

Groups connect people with a similar interest and include shared discussion threads and other tools. Some Groups require verification to join, but you do not have to be connected to everyone in the group.

Q&A

In LinkedIn's Q&A section, you can post questions to your network of connections. You can also answer questions posted by friends and colleagues on the site. Answering questions is a great way to demonstrate your expertise in a given area.

Status Update

As on Twitter and Facebook, you can write a quick post to update your network of connections on what's happening with your business. LinkedIn users can also set their Twitter accounts to Feed their LinkedIn status updates.

TWITTER

Twitter (http://twitter.com) is the social media network based on 140-character micro-blog posts. Users post short updates that can be seen by anyone, even if they are not logged into the site. Posts can include text, links, and photographs (which appear as links). The people who follow you will see your updates in their timeline when they log in. Unlike on Facebook, you do not have to confirm or reciprocate the follower connection, meaning that people can follow your updates without you having to see theirs.

@mention, see "Handle"

Direct Message (DM)

A DM, or direct message, is a private note between two users on Twitter. The intended recipient must follow the sender, and the message is bound by Twitter's 140-character limit.

Follow

To connect with other users on Twitter, you "follow" them. People who have elected to follow you will see your tweets in their timeline. You are not obligated to follow people back and you have the ability to block followers (usually spammers) from seeing your posts.

Following

If you're "following" someone on Twitter, you'll see their tweets in your own timeline. Follow people and companies in order to hear their latest updates.

Handle

Your Twitter username is referred to as your handle, and is identified with the @ symbol. For example, Constant Contact's handle is @constantcontact. My handle is @Gail_Goodman. The @ directs your tweet to the user you're referencing. For example, if you wanted to reference Constant Contact within a tweet, you would use our handle in your post.

Here's an advanced tip that many people don't know: When you use an @ reference as the first word in a tweet, only those who follow you and the user you're referencing will see the tweet. If you want all of your followers to see a tweet that references another user, use another word or character, such as a period, prior to the @ reference (e.g., ".@constantcontact").

Hashtags

Another way to get major traction with Twitter is to use hashtags. Words preceded by a # sign (i.e., #ctctsocial or #engmkt) relate your tweet to a topic, trend, or event, such as a conference, TV show, or sporting event.

If you're watching the big game or attending a conference, you can follow what others are saying about that event by searching for the relevant hashtag. If you're hosting your own event, designate a hashtag for everyone to use. Twitter automatically links all hashtags so you can easily follow the discussion. Sometimes the Twitter discussion is more fun than the actual event! (Also see "Live Tweeting.")

Lists

Lists combine select people you follow on Twitter into a smaller Feed. A list can be made up of friends, competitors, people in the same state, or anyone you want. Lists let you view a slice of your followers at a time, so they're a great way to focus on specific folks when you're following a large number of people.

Live-Tweeting

Live-tweeting is the practice of documenting an event through tweets that are posted while the event is in progress usually using a hashtag (e.g., #sxsw).

Photo sites

In order to share photos on Twitter, you have to upload them somewhere and link to them. Sites like twitpic.com, yfrog.com, and tweetphoto.com are all popular for quickly uploading and sharing pictures on Twitter. You can use the links to these photos on other sites outside of Twitter.

Retweet/RT

Retweeting is the Twitter equivalent of sharing a Facebook post or forwarding an e-mail to a friend. When someone posts content you find interesting, you can retweet it and share it with all the people who follow you. Posts that are retweets generally begin with "RT" (i.e., RT @constantcontact).

Search

Since the majority of tweets are public, you can use Twitter's search feature to look for tweets containing a keyword, phrase, or hashtag. The search results will update in real time with any new tweets that contain that word or phrase. (This is an example of "real-time search.")

Timeline

A timeline is the chronological listing of all tweets in a given Feed, be it your own, in one of your lists (see also "Lists"), or another user's.

Trending Topics

Along the right side of the main web interface, Twitter lists 10 "hot" topics of the moment based on certain algorithms. You can view trending topics for all of Twitter or for certain geographic areas. Beware: trending topics are sometimes "gamed" by people trying to promote pop culture references that aren't truly trending topics. And some businesses now pay for their product to be a trending topic (Disney was one of the first, for *Toy Story 3*).

Tweet

On Twitter, all posts are called "tweets."

Tweetup

"Tweetup" refers to an event or meetup that springs from Twitter connections. Tweetups are typically informal gatherings for Twitter followers to meet in real life. Coordinators often use a hashtag to unite tweets related to the event.

Twitterverse

"Twitterverse" is a fun term used to describe the world of Twitter.

Unfollow

If you unfollow someone, you will no longer receive their updates in your own timeline.

ENGAGEMENT MARKETING TOOLS

In this section you'll find tools to help you easily manage your Engagement Marketing efforts. Yes, we've included Constant Contact's tools. Not selling here, just informing.

Bitly

Bitly (https://bitly.com) generates short URLs that can be used for posting links on Twitter (and other sites where users are limited to specific character lengths). Users paste the long URL into a text box and the site generates a shorter replacement. The service is free, but businesses can sign up for an account that will allow them to create a more personalized short URL. For example, Constant Contact links are shortened to http://conta.cc. Other URL shortener websites include tinyurl.com, ow.ly, and is.gd.

Facebook Join My List App

With this handy app (http://apps.facebook.com/ctctjmml), your Facebook fans can sign up for your Constant Contact mailing list straight from your Page. The app has everything you need, including graphics and the subscription form. All you need is to do is add an enticement.

EdgeRank Checker

This free tool helps you increase follower engagement and exposure within Facebook. You can check your score in one simple step: Just click the "connect now for your free score" banner on the EdgeRank Checker home page (http://edgerankchecker .com).

Foursquare

Foursquare (https://foursquare.com) is a geolocation service that allows users to check in at businesses and other locations, earning badges and other virtual rewards along the way. Users can share their check-ins with fellow Foursquare friends as well as through other social media networks. Businesses can use Foursquare to identify their regular customers and offer them special deals. Another popular check-in service is Gowalla (recently acquired by Facebook). Many of the social networks are also adding check-in functionality.

Google Alerts

Google Alerts (www.google.com/alerts) allow users to save specific searches and receive an update whenever a new search result appears on the Internet. These "alerts" are typically delivered by e-mail or RSS. Google Alerts are particularly useful for businesses or organizations that wish to monitor online mentions of their brands or leaders.

HootSuite

HootSuite (http://hootsuite.com) allows businesses, organizations, and individuals to monitor, manage, and schedule their social media marketing activity.

NutshellMail

A free Constant Contact service, NutshellMail (http://nutshellmail .com) keeps track of all the happenings on your Facebook, Twitter, and LinkedIn accounts and e-mails you a digest of updates on a schedule that you choose. This service eliminates the need to keep checking into Facebook 20 times a day—an important consideration for busy business owners! All the latest updates are right there in your in-box for you to read on your own time.

Pagemodo

This handy tool (www.pagemodo.com) makes it easy to design and customize your Facebook Page. Features include developing Like-gates, adding photos and videos, and apps for coupons, contact forms, and maps.

Social Campaigns

A new service from Constant Contact, Social Campaigns (www .constantcontact.com/social-campaigns) makes it easy for your business to get more fans, so *you* can get more business. Integrated tools and coaching help you create Facebook campaigns that engage your existing audience as well as new fans.

Social Oomph

Similar to HootSuite and TweetDeck, Social Oomph (www .socialoomph.com) lets you schedule and manage your Twitter and Facebook posts.

Sprout Social

This tool (http://sproutsocial.com) lets you monitor conversations about your brand or industry across the major platforms, blogs, articles, and competitor insights and delivers robust analytics to your dashboard.

TweetDeck

A service (http://www.tweetdeck.com) that allows businesses, organizations, and individuals to monitor, manage, and schedule their social media marketing activity.

Twitpic

This handy tool (http://twitpic.com) allows you to share photos or videos on Twitter in real time. You can post media to Twitpic from your phone, from Twitter, or through e-mail.

GLOSSARY

In this section you'll find a list of terms used throughout the book as they relate to Engagement Marketing.

Aggregator   A web-based tool or application that collects syndicated content.

App   Short for Application, this is a program or add-on, usually for Facebook or for a mobile device (i.e., an iPhone or Black-Berry). Its purpose is to deepen user interaction and provide greater depth of functionality and engagement. For example, Facebook has created apps for the iPhone and Android phone to enhance the mobile Facebook experience.

Comments   Many social media sites encourage readers and viewers to leave comments on content that others have posted, whether that content is a quick status message, a video, an article, or a picture. Some sites, like Facebook, use the number of comments to determine the placement of a post in a user's News Feed. On YouTube, video "owners" have the ability to turn off comments for an individual video.

Crowdsource   Crowdsourcing is the practice of asking a collection of individuals online for opinions, suggestions, or submissions. For example, if you can't choose between two articles for the company newsletter, ask the people who Like you on Facebook or follow you on Twitter which one you should include.

Or you could simply post both stories to Facebook and Twitter to discover which one resonates more with your audience based on the number of Likes, shares, comments, or retweets. Crowdsourcing can also be helpful if you're planning an event and can't decide on a date or location, or if you're looking for suggestions for a vendor.

Explicit Endorsements   A positive recommendation or review about your business is an explicit endorsement. People can endorse your business on a review site or social media platform. These endorsements can also take the form of a testimonial or case study for your website. Explicit endorsements help boost your site higher on review sites, such as TripAdvisor, and they also carry social proof.

Engaged   People who interact with a business, organization, or individual online by posting comments and sharing content are said to be engaged. (Also see "Lurker.")

Engagement Marketing/Engagement Marketing Cycle   Engagement Marketing is the process of encouraging your clients and customers to tell your story for you through socially visible word-of-mouth referrals. These referrals are noticed by your customers and their friends, families, and networks, leading even more people to your business.

The Engagement Marketing Cycle is comprised of three steps: Provide a WOW! experience, entice people to keep in touch with you, and engage people through content they'll want to share with their networks.

Implied Endorsement   Endorsement is implied when someone engages with your business by commenting, Liking, tagging, or checking in on social networks. Because we usually engage with businesses we like, this engagement carries with it a positive or implied endorsement.

Lurker A lurker is a social network user who simply listens and watches but doesn't participate in conversations or activities on the site.

Network Network can refer to a social network, such as Facebook, Twitter, or LinkedIn, or the people you're connected to on those sites.

Preferred Destination A preferred destination is the main place to which you want to drive social traffic. This destination can be your blog, Facebook Page, or even your e-newsletter. Having a preferred destination helps you gain traction in one place (and helps you avoid getting overwhelmed) as it's better to have 100 fans or followers on one platform versus 25 of them on each of the four networks.

RSS RSS literally stands for Really Simple Syndication. An RSS Feed allows the content from regularly updated websites such as blogs or podcasts to be aggregated and posted to one website (often called a "reader") or mobile device. Choosing to follow an RSS feed is often referred to as "subscribing" to the Feed.

Share To post or repost content on a social media site is to share it. Facebook, LinkedIn, and Google+ each have a share option, which allows you to post someone else's content on your Page. On Twitter, sharing is called retweeting.

Share Button/Bar You can add a share button or bar to your website, blog, or e-newsletter so that your content can be easily shared on social media sites. AddThis (http://addthis.com) offers popular, free share buttons and bars.

Social Media Platforms such as Facebook, Twitter, LinkedIn, Google+, and Foursquare allow the sharing of information and creation of communities through online networks of people.

Social Media Marketing Building your social network connections using relevant and interesting content that is shared allows you to reach and engage more people and drive more business.

Social Networks   The social media sites (i.e., Facebook, Twitter, LinkedIn, Google+) where people connect and interact with friends, colleagues, businesses, and organizations are called social networks.

Social Proof   Social proof is a "psychological phenomenon where people assume the actions of others reflect the correct behavior for a given situation." If your friend Bob eats at a restaurant and posts positively about it on Facebook, you're now predisposed to eat at the same restaurant. This is because you value Bob's opinion and judgment, so if Bob did it and liked it, it must be good.

Social proof comes in five types: Expert, Celebrity, User, Wisdom of the Crowds, and Wisdom of Your Friends. This last one is most relevant to Engagement Marketing and has been deemed by experts to be the "killer app" that's still relatively untapped. (See Chapter 5 for a full discussion of social proof.)

Socially Visible Call-to-Action   Calls-to-action tell people what to do next: Like our Page, answer a poll question, or download something, for example. Socially visible calls-to-action are those actions that show up in your fans' friends' Feeds: shares, photo tags, and check-ins. See Social Visibility below.

Social Visibility   Actions people take on social platforms that expose their friends to your business are considered socially visible. For example, sharing content is a socially visible action. When your fans share, this action appears in their friends' Feeds—which means that people who may not have known about your business are exposed to your content.

Viral   When a piece of content on the Internet is shared organically, without prodding or encouragement from the business, organization, or person who created it, it is said to have "gone viral." This means it has been shared on social networks, posted and reposted, tweeted and retweeted multiple times.

About the Author

Gail F. Goodman is the CEO of Constant Contact, a leading provider of e-mail marketing, social media marketing, and event marketing and online survey tools for small organizations.

A small business expert and visionary, Gail has revolutionized the way small businesses and organizations can effectively and affordably build relationships with their customers, clients, and members. Since taking leadership of Constant Contact in April 1999, she has led the company to its initial public offering on the NASDAQ in October 2007 and more than half a million customers worldwide.

Gail was named "Executive of the Year" at the 2009 American Business Awards and was the 2008 New England Regional winner of Ernst & Young's Entrepreneur of the Year. In 2011, she was inducted into the MITX Innovation Hall of Fame and named one of Boston's Top 30 Innovators by *The Boston Globe*. Under her leadership, Constant Contact was ranked number 179 on Deloitte's 2011 Technology Fast 500 and was named Best Overall Company at the 2009, 2010, and 2011 American Business Awards.

Along the way, Gail has worked with and talked with literally thousands of small businesses and organizations. Through the years, she has learned a variety of lessons on how small businesses succeed in reaching and keeping customers—all of which she brings to bear in *Engagement Marketing*.

A frequent speaker at industry events, Gail develops and tracks best practices in small business success; e-mail, event, and social media marketing; customer communications; and entrepreneurship. Gail is a member of the Board of Trustees of the Massachusetts Technology Leadership Council, a member of the Board of Directors of SCORE, and Chairman of the Board at Constant Contact.

Gail holds a BA from The University of Pennsylvania and an MBA from The Tuck School of Business at Dartmouth College.

ACKNOWLEDGMENTS

Many people helped me with the creation of this book. I would especially like to thank the team at John Wiley & Sons, Inc. Thanks to Anita Campbell for sharing her insights about small business in the Foreword, and to Eric Groves for helping to develop the concepts of *Engagement Marketing*.

I'd also like to thank all of the members of the Constant Contact team who helped bring this book to life, including Erica Ayotte, Melissa Ayres, Dave Charest, Liz Fischer, Katie Healey, Blaise Lucey, and Brian McDonald. A very special thank you to Dianna Huff. And a big shout-out to my husband, Dave Swindell, for his love, support, and understanding.

INDEX

E-newsletters, also e-mail
newsletters (*continued*)
Maas Nursery's example,
118–119
Subscription form, 42
EdgeRank checker, 157–158, 176
Employees
customer experience skills of,
25–26
empowerment, customer care
experience, 25–26
enlisting for Engagement
Marketing help, 151
photos of in e-newsletters, 121
Endorsements, 76–78, 180
Engaged
customers, 80
defined, 180
discussions, 56, 75
Facebook, 112, 159
quantify, 47
surveys, 94–95
Engagement
announcements, 59–63
calls to action, 65–67
defined, 11, 49
endorsements through, 76–78
events, 63–65
goal of, 11–12
marketing enhancements by,
78–79
promotions, 59–63
prospects, 79–80
purpose of, 13, 50
quality focus of, 70–72, 146–147

social visibility and, 13–14,
74–75
tools for, 50–51, 175–178
Engagement Marketing
basic idea of, 5
characterization of, 33
defined, 180
overcoming common obstacles,
146–159
resources, 161–178
tips and tricks, 133–143
tools, 175–179
engagementmarketing.com, 95,
131, 148, 161
Engagement Marketing cycle
building momentum with, 14–15
circle of influence, 4–5
closing loop of, 12
commencement of, 6–7
components of, 85–86
defined, 180
momentum, 14
new business engine, 6
social visibility, new prospects, 13
stages of, 8–12
steps to success, 7
support sales and marketing, 14
Enticements
creation of, 153–154
focus, 39–40
Gourmet Coffee Service
example of, 108–109
initiation of, 10
methods of, 34
nonprofits, 35–36